MW01286915

How to Become a Corporate Board Member

By Ade Asefeso MCIPS MBA

First Edition

ISBN-13: 978-1515149682

ISBN-10: 1515149684

Publisher: AA Global Sourcing Ltd
Website: http://www.aaglobalsourcing.com

Table of Contents

Disclaimer...5

Dedication...6

Chapter 1: Introduction 7

Chapter 2: The New Vision of Corporate Board Membership. 13

Chapter 3: Behind Boardroom Doors. 19

Chapter 4: Things You Need to Do to Become a Corporate Board Member. 23

Chapter 5: The Role of a Director. 27

Chapter 6: Board of Directors Responsibility and Structure. 31

Chapter 7: Roles and Responsibilities of the Non-profit Board. 37

Chapter 8: Should I Be a Director?....................43

Chapter 9: Questions About Boards....................47

Chapter 10: Six Steps to Getting a Place on the Board...55

Chapter 11: How to Get On a Corporate Board. .59

Chapter 12: Steps to Becoming a Corporate Director. 61

Chapter 13: Landing a Seat On a Corporate Board. 65

Chapter 14: What It Takes to Get On Board........69

Chapter 15: Joining Boards: It's Not Just Who You Know That Matters. 73

Chapter 16: Women in the Boardroom................77

Chapter 17: Why Women Over 50 Should Join Non-profit Boards. 81

Chapter 18: How to Find a Rewarding Non-profit Board Position. 85

Chapter 19: Essential Elements of Board-Building. 95

Chapter 20: Board Effectiveness. 99

Chapter 21: Building a High Performing Fully Actualized Board. 105

Chapter 22: Barriers to Board Effectiveness in Non-profit Organisation. 109

Chapter 23: Non-profit Organisation's Board Development Process. 113

Chapter 24: Non-profit Organisation's Board Committee Structure. 121

Chapter 25: Non-profit Organisation's Annual Board Self-evaluation Process. 125

Chapter 26: Building an Effective Non-profit Board of Directors. 129

Chapter 27: Summary of Roles and Responsibilities of Directors and Boards 131

Chapter 28: Conclusion 139

Disclaimer

This publication is designed to provide competent and reliable information regarding the subject matter covered. However, it is sold with the understanding that the author and publisher are not engaged in rendering professional advice. The authors and publishers specifically disclaim any liability that is incurred from the use or application of contents of this book.

If you purchased this book without a cover you should be aware that this book may have been stolen property and reported as "unsold and destroyed" to the publisher. In this case neither the author nor the publisher has received any payment for this "stripped book."

Dedication

To my family and friends who seems to have been sent here to teach me something about who I am supposed to be. They have nurtured me, challenged me, and even opposed me.... But at every juncture has taught me!

This book is dedicated to my lovely boys, Thomas, Michael and Karl. Teaching them to manage their finance will give them the lives they deserve. They have taught me more about life, presence, and energy management than anything I have done in my life.

Chapter 1: Introduction

There has always been a certain mystique about how corporate boards are constructed. In broad terms, corporate boards are guided by the bylaws set in place to oversee and approve annual budgets, make sure there are adequate resources to run operations, elect the chief executives and provide general oversight on behalf of shareholders and any entity with a stake in the company. The board is also responsible for verifying the availability of future capital-raising sources and reviewing the business practices of their most senior leaders. The board's most important duty is keeping tabs of the company in all matters including performance, relative and absolute delivery of direction and the decision to fire CEOs when needed.

Board members of companies are rarely thrust into the spotlight, especially when companies have kept pace with their industry's competitors, delivered profitable quarters and, ultimately, rewards to shareholders in the forms of dividends and capital appreciation. With so many companies having been caught in illegal or unethical scandals over the past few decades, the board's responsibility has been called into question by the investing public. There has also been a sense of an old-boy-network, as most boards have had an almost monopoly on who is placed on the ballot before the proxy materials are sent to shareholders. The process for nominating board member candidates has become more investor-friendly, opening up the playing field while still maintaining the original concept of having that extra layer of oversight.

Where Boards Come From

The most important role for any corporate board is to provide a level of oversight between those who manage a company and those who own the company, whether it's public shareholders or private investors. Most boards are comprised of high-level managers and executives of other companies, academics and some professional board members who sit on multiple boards. Historically, board members nominate, via proxy mailings, candidates who they feel will best suit the needs of the company rather than from a pool of shareholders. Some say the construction of boards, by its very nature, creates an almost disinterested party as there is not much incentive for boards to get too involved and many have been accused of voting with management. In addition, board members are rarely held directly responsible for company failures and scandals. Part of this is due to the fact that their powers to actually run the company are limited, and after their terms they just move on to the next appointment.

Political oversight and regulations like the Sarbanes-Oxley Act of 2002 (SOX) have been developed partially in response to some of the most famous large scale company failures and scandals, like Enron and WorldCom, which cost investors billions of dollars. So far, while not lacking it share of sceptics, SOX has raised the bar for high-level managers and CEOs who are now accountable in writing for the information they present to the Securities and Exchange Commission (SEC) and their shareholders. As for the construction of corporate boards, very little changes have been made, but the SEC has adopted a new set of procedures for the nomination of potential board candidates.

The Problem for Investors

The problems shareholders have argued for as long as there have been boards is that only current board members or a separate nominating committee can nominate new board candidates, and this information is passed along to investors in the proxy materials. During the nomination period, shareholders have little or no say in the process, and their choice for board nominations have little or no chance of getting on the ballot prior to proxy release. Most investors, including institutional holders, find it more convenient to vote for the candidate presented to them in the proxy materials rather than attend the annual shareholders' meeting and vote personally. In fact, most investment groups have dedicated teams for this purpose alone.

Since shareholders in most situations have to attend shareholders' meetings in order to nominate their own candidates, you don't have to be anti-big-business to see the apparent flaws in the current system and the SEC has stepped up with a permanent change in the process.

What Investors Can Do

On August 25, 2010, the SEC passed a rule that allows investors and shareholders to nominate board members by placing them on the proxy ballot mailings before they are mailed out. To limit an overflow in nominations, there is a 3% ownership requirement for individuals or groups, but investors are taking action that will forever change how investors are represented. In a simplified application, just about anyone can successfully nominate themselves via the proxy system, and if they receive enough votes they join the board. Investors and their advocate groups of all sizes are looking for a permanent overhaul and a new level of representation and board accountability.

Benefits, Changes and the SEC

While a nomination on a proxy ballot by no means guarantees an elected seat, the potential benefits for shareholders are monumental.

1. Shareholders with the desire, resources and time can access the nomination process once held only by current boards.
2. Shareholder groups, from large influential pension funds to small groups, can now back their own candidates.
3. Shareholders will have a much closer relationship with boards.
4. Accountability will increase dramatically, as nominees become elected and results are expected.

Shareholder advocates look for the following characteristics in a board;

1. No more of the old-boy network where old boards essentially control who replaces them through nominations.
2. New corporate boards that are actually shareholders who want to help shape the company's direction.
3. The arrival of the representation by those outside of an Ivory Tower.
4. The eventual composition of a board that has no interest in just voting with management because they are influenced in some way.
5. The elimination of the "professional board members" who sit on multiple boards.
6. Higher turnover at the board level as shareholders nominate and vote in their choices.
7. Potentially higher levels of transparency and ultimately accountability.

The SEC, and most government-related agencies, have not had the best of press throughout the 2000s, regardless of political party or responsibility. While the Financial Industry Regulatory Authority (FINRA) has escaped much criticism, the SEC has been accused of letting shenanigans and even crimes carry on for years. While most of the criticism has been of the agency in general, one of the most publicized cases was the Bernie Madoff scam, which cost large and small investors billions. Because the SEC had actually visited and "audited" Madoff's operations and had received various complaints and accusations, this left the SEC with a bit of a black eye. This proxy process change is one of many ideas the SEC has put in motion to present itself as a more investor-friendly group rather than some of the negative views many have expressed of them.

The process of board construction has been on the wish list of shareholders for a long time, and the companies they may eventually influence are not as responsive to the process. This will inevitably mean higher administrative and legal costs to all companies big and small. While large companies will probably see less influence, once shareholders start flooding the proxy process, costs are destined to rise. It will take years to see significant changes as the rulings phase in, but it looks like the SEC is becoming a little more investor responsive, and soon anyone will have the opportunity to join that elite group of board of directors!

Chapter 2: The New Vision of Corporate Board Membership.

In the past, joining a corporate board conjured visions of networking at posh resorts with politicians and celebrities. People used to look at board membership as a cushy way of making a lot of money up until the millennium. What was important for very large, high visibility boards was having star names on them; celebrities, political people, anybody who would give a halo effect to say how important your company was; but those days are over. A 2002 law imposing stringent new corporate requirements, board membership has become a tightly regulated, formal affair. Searches are often handled by professional search firms. The definition of qualified has significantly been altered. There are very clear regulations for independent directors in terms of the credentials necessary to be a financial expert or compensation expert. You need to demonstrate proof in past experiences, degrees, focus, and the skill sets board members bring.

So if you are not a former Fortune 500 CFO or CEO, how can you make yourself a credible candidate for a corporate board seat? First, develop and leverage the right professional skills. The best background for any board at this time is probably having a financial background and being available to sit on the audit committee. Also, a hot area right now is that everybody wants a social media expert to help inform them.

Now it's time to seek out experience on actual boards. Non-profit boards serve as a great launching pad for corporate board service. Be sure to seek a seat on the Board of Trustees with fiduciary responsibility, rather than serving on an advisory board. Start-up or private company boards may also be a good starting point. It's often easier to get on non-public company boards; people view those as critical foundational experiences.

The next step is ensuring that interested companies can find you. People need to be more visible in raising their hand for board work; they have to put themselves out there instead of waiting for the world to come to them. Aspiring board members may want to attend events held by the National Association of Corporate Directors, which are frequently open to interested members of the public. All of the big search firms that have board practices have websites that you can post your resume on; if you have a unique skill set or industry knowledge, it's a great way of getting the door open. You should reach out to your colleagues who are already board members; it's fine to call people you know who sit on boards and say, "Here is my skill set, I have got experience in this industry, I am a financial expert, I am a compensation expert; how do I find a board in this industry or with this kind of need?"

It is critical to recognize the intense time commitment corporate board service requires. You are going to have telephone committee meetings, there may be a crisis, or suddenly you need to vote on something. Be prepared to be sequestered with your board if there is a crisis and think carefully if you don't have a job that tolerates it or a life that can allow it.

Winning a corporate board seat isn't easy. But if you have the right skills and pursue opportunities assiduously, it can be a powerful way to accelerate your career and make a contribution.

We must not forget that the board of directors is the heart of an organization. The members make tough decisions such as hiring a CEO, mapping out a financial plan and maintaining ethics. Being a member on the board of directors offers benefits such as increased responsibility, enhanced experience and extra recognition. For others, it is rewarding to assist in the success of the business, organization or non-profit that they have always cared about. The admission process and competition for becoming a member on the board of directors can be intense therefore you have to.

1. Become a well-known figure in your community to begin to expand your support base during the voting, nomination or appointment season for choosing a new member for the board of directors. Attend, sponsor and speak at events. Look in the newspaper for book clubs, wine tasting socials, museum showings and political campaigns. Make an effort to get connected to recognized and renowned community leaders by networking, then contacting them and offering to assist them in their endeavours. Over time you will become influential in your community and establish a solid reputation.

2. Play an important role in your community and with the business, non-profit or organization that you wish to join the board of directors. Do this through philanthropy work, becoming a consistent donor to the organization, participating actively in associations, being an avid volunteer, becoming a leader in your industry or becoming a public servant. These positions give you experience and enable you to demonstrate your credibility, earn accolades and show exceptional judgment.

3. Focus on developing a relationship with the business, organization or non-profit that you are interested in. Attend its open meetings, volunteer, donate to its cause and otherwise show that you genuinely care about the organization's mission. Have a friendly personality with a warm smile and thoughtful gifts; build trust through conversation and giving members of your target organization information about resources that could significantly assist them.

4. On the application, showcase your knowledge of the organization, non-profit or business and display your understanding of financial and management matters. You will learn about the business, non-profit or organization by volunteering for them, using their services, doing extensive research and getting to know the owners and staff. To brush up on your management and financial skills, go to seminars and take business administration courses at a local collage. In your daily life, work on budgeting and managing relations.

5. Become well-connected with the current board of directors to improve your chances of being approved as a member. Find where the board of directors frequent, talk to the board of directors after meetings, get to know the current candidates for board of directors and find out the partnerships that the board of directors have. Often these partnerships will co-sponsor events and other widespread efforts, so participate actively in these events.

6. During your interactions with the board of directors and on the application, show your unique traits and skills that would make you a valuable asset to the board of the directors. Excel in your volunteer work and in your personal life, then give anecdotes on how you were able to predict trends and make sound economic decisions that caused growth in your business or at your job. Learn how to fundraise by assisting fundraisers, or attend grant writing sessions so that you will be able to share the amount of funds you have been able to secure.

7. Boost your team work and leadership personality traits by putting yourself in situations that demand these qualities, such as organizations and leadership roles. If you don't become a member the first time you apply, use this as motivation. Be positive and realize that you are now more familiar with the process.

8. Be sure to maintain all new contacts and commitments to prevent losing touch and seeming unreliable. Unethical or corrupt practices in your

personal life have the potential of barring you from becoming a member on the board of directors.

Chapter 3: Behind Boardroom Doors.

It takes a team to build a successful venture. A company's board of directors is the ultimate team that accepts the overall responsibility for the firm. Unfortunately, even if you hang together, and something goes wrong, each director may be held singularly accountable both to the shareholders and to the general public.

Board composition and behaviour.

Highly effective boards include a mix of directors with the expertise and experience to fulfil their essential oversight roles. Directors' responsibilities are expanding, and the number and complexity of the issues they have to oversee are increasing.

Having a board made up of the right people with the relevant skill sets is critical in today's competitive business environment. But how do boards get that dynamic in place? It starts with finding bright director candidates with the right array of skills and experience. In today's ever-changing business world, it's no surprise that industry and financial expertise are the most valued attributes by directors. As more companies embrace emerging technologies and new strategies leveraging technology, boards are also seeking directors with digital skills. Three-quarters say technology and digital media expertise is at least somewhat important, an increase from 68% a year earlier.

The average corporate board has 10 people, and the average director sits on a board for just over eight and a half years. What if someone on the board isn't measuring up? More than one in three directors (35%) think someone on their board should be replaced. The top three reasons are diminished performance because of aging, a lack of the required expertise, and poor preparation for meetings. Over half of directors who have served on the board less than one year believe a fellow board member should be replaced but fewer than 25% who have served more than 10 years feel the same. The biggest hurdles to replacing an underperforming colleague lie with board leadership's discomfort addressing the issue, followed by a lack of individual director assessments.

The ideal board,

An ideal board is one which works closely with the Chief Executive Officer (the "CEO") of the company to give not only support and direction to him or her, but one which also challenges the CEO to make sure that he or she leads the company in accordance with the company's plans. Many boards are "puppet" boards often play along with the CEO and management. These are useless. The board should be the pillar which holds the company up. The board is responsible for the success or failure of the company. Furthermore, it is the soul and conscience of the enterprise. If management is not doing its job that is because the board is not doing its job in the first instance. The mandate of the CEO, guided by an active board, is to drive the value of the company. A board serves the company not specific shareholders or groups.

When companies first begin, the shareholders, managers, and board members are all one and the same. For example, if a few people launch a new business, they will all be the initial shareholders, managers, and directors. As they evolve, these three groupings of company participants may diverge with respect to the people involved in each category. The shareholders own the company and they appoint the directors who in turn appoint the managers. When companies raise capital by attracting new investors, these new shareholders will, with the current shareholders, want to make sure that their interests are served by a competent board of directors. Many private companies operate like partnerships, i.e. the people who run the company also own it and govern it without involving any outsiders. On the other hand, there is a trend by shareholders; regardless of number to attract external, independent people to serve as corporate directors, thereby contributing expertise and oversight and a "big picture" perspective. In larger, public corporations, the only manager on the board is the company's CEO. Directors are generally also shareholders in the company; this aligns their interests with other shareholders whom they serve.

Chapter 4: Things You Need to Do to Become a Corporate Board Member.

Being a corporate board member has its share of great perks. Financially, it pays a lot. Board members of the 500 leading publicly traded companies in the U.S. Market, as listed in the S&P 500 Index, received over an average of $251,000 in 2014. The average pay for directors is almost six times the $42,700 average salary for private-sector workers holding down full-time jobs. That is roughly 1,789 hours of work, as opposed to the 250 to 300 hours rendered by board members in a year. Board members are paid big money for their insight gained from years of experience, something that not many people have.

The benefits of being a board member go beyond money. It's also an excellent way to network with and learn from industry leaders and other influential people and of course, board membership is a badge of honour in itself. When someone receives an invitation to join a board, it means that an organization recognizes his or her expertise. Socially and professionally, board membership is quite a lucrative venture.

There used to be a time when board members were picked because of their status. Big names were popular choices because they generated buzz, giving organizations the publicity they wanted. People who had the necessary skills, experiences, and wisdom to be board members were not necessarily invited if they were not well-known enough within their industries.

After the financial scandals in the early part of the millennium, it became obvious that tighter corporate governance was needed to protect the interests of shareholders. As mentioned earlier in this book Sarbanes-Oxley Act was passed in the U.S, a law that requires public companies and accounting firms to adhere to stricter standards when making corporate disclosures, such as earnings and losses. As a result, organizations became more careful in choosing truly qualified board members. Also, board members are expected to take an active role in spotting and eliminating fraudulent activities; otherwise, they have the law to answer to.

Because of the rewards and responsibilities that come with being a board member, not just anybody can land a seat on a board. But if you are a CEO, VP, or C-suite executive, you are on the right track because you are already working closely with your organization's board. Some companies don't allow their CEOs to sit on their boards, but if your company doesn't have that kind of restriction, express your interest in getting a seat, especially if you get along well with your board members. If you have a good working relationship with your board's members, chances are that they will be supportive of you.

But if your relationship with them is not as strong as you want it to be, you can improve it by actively working with them. Share your ideas, ask questions, participate in discussions; not only will these get you on board members' radar, but they will also help you be more effective at your job.

Making connections is effective not just for within your organization, but for others as well if you want to expand your options, networking plays a big role in getting tapped for a board seat. You have to fish where the fish are; if you know you wanted to be a board member, you should take on a proactive role by getting to know CEOs and directors. You should not sit around and wait for the invitations to arrive; that will come later on, after you had already made a reputation for yourself. But for that crucial first board seat, you may have to go cold calling industry vendors and asked them to send in proxy votes for you.

You should not stop there, though. After creating contacts, you should build relationships with people by spending time with them and finding out what made them tick. In many ways, getting a board seat is part industry expertise, part public relations skills.

But what if you are not a CEO, VP, or C-suite executive? It may be harder for you to become a board member, but it's not impossible. There are two things you need to accomplish to get a shot at becoming a board member: Do your job exceptionally well, and reach out to people. It's a simple recipe for success, but it's not an easy one; nevertheless, it could all worth it in the end.

Chapter 5: The Role of a Director.

Typically, a director is (or should be) a shareholder in the company. Directors are appointed, i.e. voted into office, by the shareholders of a company at a properly convened meeting of shareholders. The number of directors of a company is determined by a special resolution of shareholders, which number can be changed only by a shareholder vote (although boards can fill vacancies and make minor changes to board composition). In general, shareholders will appoint themselves as directors (as is the case for small companies) or will vote on a slate of nominees proposed by any shareholder(s). Certain shareholders, by virtue of a shareholders' agreement or voting trust, may have the right to appoint directors to a board. The directors are accountable to all shareholders and must act in the best interests of the company. Furthermore, directors are not protected by those that appoint them.

Additionally, directors have a legal obligation to ensure that a company is operated in a proper, legal, good-corporate-citizen style. If a company's products blow up in the face of a consumer, or if a company fails to remit taxes, it is the directors that are held liable and they may be personally sued. For this reason, many companies will subscribe for liability insurance and will also indemnify directors against such actions. But, the directors may still be exposed. In a spectacular, case involving Canadian Airlines, the entire board resigned from office because the airline was on the verge of financial disaster in which case the directors would jointly and severally be responsible for employee wages and taxes owing by the airline.

The time commitment of a directorship should not be underestimated. Even though your board may only sit formally once a month or once each quarter, as a director you must know what is going on all the time. You can never use the excuse that you weren't told about something. You will likely also be asked to serve on board committees (compensation committee, audit committee, executive committee, etc.). A good chief executive will use his board wisely seeking counsel and advice regularly and will keep his board fully informed on major issues.

In the case of public companies, a reputable board comprised of objective, "outside" directors is seen to be a plus in the eyes of investors. These outside directors, often referred to as the "independent" directors because they are independent of management are supposed to hold management accountable for corporate actions and serve in the best interests of the company. Often, shareholders' interests are at odds with those of management. For example, paying huge management bonuses or being excessively generous with stock options may be good for managers while reducing shareholder value. Having a slate of independent directors shows that the company has good leadership and at the same time, that these leaders are willing to assume the potential personal liabilities required to make the company successful.

Directors are very powerful. They often do not even understand the extent of this power. A director, dissatisfied about some management action, could call a board meeting to deal with the matter. He or she needn't wait for the next scheduled meeting. A director may sign important legal documents on behalf of a company making onerous commitments on behalf of that company. A company's officers, especially the President and CEO, are appointed by, and accountable to, the directors.

Directing versus Managing.

Directing is not the same as managing. Directors make sure that managers are doing the managing and that the company is recruiting the necessary talent for this purpose. Directors hold management accountable. It is a good practice to have directors require that management produce regular updates on progress, especially in the early years. For start-ups a weekly reporting system is not uncommon. In the case of young companies, directors often become quite involved in day to day matters and sometimes they assume a part-time management role as well. Directors work with management to approve budgets, business plans, senior job descriptions, compensation, policies, and financial statements. With respect to job descriptions, it is advisable to draw up some "terms of reference" for a board which clearly articulate not only legal duties and responsibilities but also any other expectations.

Chapter 6: Board of Directors Responsibility and Structure.

Mention the phrase "board of directors" to the average investor, and they are likely to conjure up images of nicely dressed men and women standing around a mahogany table, smiling congenially. This is entirely understandable; many annual reports prominently feature glossy photographs of just such a scene. Now, ask the investor to describe the primary responsibility of the board of directors and very few will be able to give you a definitive answer.

Purpose, Authority and Responsibility of the Board of Directors.

The primary responsibility of the board of directors is to protect the shareholders' assets and ensure they receive a decent return on their investment. In some European countries, the sentiment is much different; many directors in Europe feel that it is their primary responsibility to protect the employees of a company first, the shareholders second. In these social and political climates, corporate profitability takes a back seat behind the needs of workers.

The board of directors is the highest governing authority within the management structure at any publicly traded company. It is the board's job to select, evaluate, and approve appropriate compensation for the company's chief executive officer (CEO), evaluate the attractiveness of and pay

31

dividends, recommend stock splits, oversee share repurchase programs, approve the company's financial statements, and recommend or strongly discourage acquisitions and mergers.

Structure and Makeup of the Board of Directors

The board is made up of individual men and women (the "directors") who are elected by the shareholders for multiple-year terms. Many companies operate on a rotating system so that only a fraction of the directors are up for election each year; this makes it much more difficult for a complete board change to take place due to a hostile takeover. In most cases, directors either, 1.) have a vested interest in the company, 2.) work in the upper management of the company, or 3.) are independent from the company but are known for their business abilities.

The number of directors can vary substantially between companies. Walt Disney, for example, has sixteen directors, each of whom are elected at the same time for one year terms. Tiffany & Company, on the other hand, has only eight directors on its board. In the United States, at least fifty percent of the directors must meet the requirements of "independence", meaning they are not associated with or employed by the company. In theory, independent directors will not be subject to pressure, and therefore are more likely to act in the shareholders' interests when those interests run counter to those of entrenched management.

Committees on the Board of Directors

The board of directors responsibilities include the establishment of the audit and compensation committees. The audit committee is responsible for ensuring that the company's financial statements and reports are accurate and use fair and reasonable estimates. The board members select, hire, and work with an outside auditing firm. The firm is the entity that actually does the auditing.

The compensation committee sets base compensation, stock option awards, and incentive bonuses for the company's executives, including the CEO. In recent years, many board of directors have come under fire for allowing executives salaries to reach unjustifiably absurd levels.

In exchange for providing their services, corporate directors are paid a yearly salary, additional compensation for each meeting they attend, stock options, and various other benefits. The total amount of directorship fees varies from company to company. When you consider that many executives sit on multiple boards, it's easy to understanding how their directorship fees can reach into the hundreds of thousands of dollars per year.

Ownership Structure and Its Impact on the Board of Directors.

The particular ownership structure of a corporation has a huge impact on the effectiveness of the board of directors to govern. In a company where a large, single shareholder exists, that entity or individual investor can effectively control the corporation. If the director has a problem, he or she can appeal to the controlling shareholder. In a company where no controlling shareholder exists, the directors should act as if one did exist and attempt to protect this imaginary entity at all times (even if it means firing the CEO, making changes to the structure that are unpopular with management, or turning down acquisitions because they are too pricey). In a relatively few number of companies, the controlling shareholder also serves as the CEO and or Chairman of the Board. In this case, a director is completely at the will of the owner and has no effective way to override his or her decisions.

Major Duties of Board of Directors

1. Provide continuity for the organization by setting up a corporation or legal existence, and to represent the organization's point of view through interpretation of its products and services, and advocacy for them.

2. Select and appoint a chief executive to whom responsibility for the administration of the organization is delegated, including:
   a) To review and evaluate his/her performance regularly on the basis of a specific job description, including executive relations with the board, leadership in the organization, in product/service/program planning and implementation, and in management of the organization and its personnel.

b) To offer administrative guidance and determine whether to retain or dismiss the executive.

3. Govern the organization by broad policies and objectives, formulated and agreed upon by the chief executive and employees, including to assign priorities and ensure the organization's capacity to carry out products/services/programs by continually reviewing its work.

4. Acquire sufficient resources for the organization's operations and to finance the products, services and programs adequately.

5. Account to the shareholders (in the case of a for-profit) or public (in the case of a non-profit) for the products and services of the organization and expenditures of its funds, including:
   a) To provide for fiscal accountability, approve the budget, and formulate policies related to contracts from public or private resources.
   b) To accept responsibility for all conditions and policies attached to new, innovative, or experimental products/services/programs.

Major Responsibilities of Board of Directors

1. Determine the organization's mission and purpose.

2. Select the executive.

3. Support the executive and review his or her performance.

4. Ensure effective organizational planning.

5. Ensure adequate resources.

6. Manage resources effectively.

7. Determine and monitor the organization's products, services and programs.

8. Enhance the organization's public image.

9. Serve as a Court of Appeal.

10. Assess its own performance.

Chapter 7: Roles and Responsibilities of the Non-profit Board.

Members of the non-profit board of directors are trustees who act on behalf of an organization's constituents, including service recipients, funders, members, the government and taxpayers. The basic responsibilities of non-profit board of directors include, but are not limited to:

1. Determining the organization's mission and purpose.

2. Supporting and evaluating the chief executive with the goals of the organization in mind.

3. Ensuring effective organizational planning.

4. Determining which of the organization's programs are consistent with its mission and monitoring the effectiveness of these programs.

5. Securing adequate financial resources for the organization to fulfil its mission.

6. Assisting in the development of the organization's annual budget and ensuring that proper financial controls are in place.

7. Defining prerequisites for potential new board members, orienting these new members, and periodically evaluating performance.

8. Adhering to legal and ethical standards and norms.

9. Clearly defining and articulating the organization's mission, accomplishments and goals to gain support from the community and enhancing the organization's public image.

10. Overall, board members have a duty of loyalty to the organization, its staff and other board members. While differences of opinion will likely arise, board members should keep disagreements impersonal. By practicing discretion and accepting decisions made on a majority basis, the board can accomplish unity and confidence in its decisions.

Non-profit board of directors should be open to self evaluation and regularly review their own composition to ensure constituent representation, board expertise and commitment. Boards also are responsible for evaluating and determining compensation for the executive director. Board members perform their responsibilities through regular meetings and a committee structure that is appropriate for the size of the board and organization. Board members are responsible for arriving at meetings well-prepared and ready to engage in thoughtful dialogue.

Legal Responsibilities of the Board of Directors.

The board is ultimately responsible for the performance of the organization in all areas of its work and should ensure that the organization is in compliance with state and federal law. The following checklist of tasks non-profits are legally required to perform is neither intended nor to be construed as legal advice.

1. Organizations with more than $25,000 in financial activity should file IRS Form 990 with the IRS. Organizations with less than $25,000 in financial activity should file the 990-N e-postcard.

2. Complete an audit if the organization's total revenue exceeds $750,000 in a year, and file the audit with the charities division of the State Attorney General's Office.

3. Report a change of name, address or amendments to the articles of incorporation to the Secretary of State and pay any necessary fees for changes.

4. Make the IRS Form 990 and Form 1023 available to the public.

5. Report any Unrelated Business Income to the State Department of Revenue and the IRS, and send tax payments with IRS Form 990T.

6. Withhold taxes from employees, and send withholding payments to the IRS.

7. Comply with laws that affect all employers, including Americans with Disabilities Act, Occupational Safety and Health Organization, Fair Labour Standards Act, Federal Insurance Contribution Acts, COBRA and Family Medical Leave Act.

8. Report any lobbying activities on the IRS Form 990, and register as a lobbyist if required.

9. Give receipts to donors for contributions over $250.

10. Collect sales tax on items sold by the organization, unless tickets are sold to performances by a performing arts organization.

11. Get court approval for distribution of assets.

12. Register with the gambling board if the organization conducts charitable gambling activities.

13. Pay property taxes or obtain an exemption from the county where the property is located, if the organization owns real property.

14. Pay regular bulk mail rate or obtain a non-profit bulk mail permit if the organization sends bulk mail.

15. Comply with the terms of donations; promises made to donors are legally binding. Funds given for specific projects or programs need to be kept separate.

16. Comply with state law regarding conflicts of interest.

17. Make sure any professional fundraisers register with the charities division of the State Attorney General's Office, and file a copy of the contract.

18. Obtain city permits for all cities in which the organization actively solicits door-to-door by paid solicitors.

19. Record minutes of board and annual meetings.

Individual Board Members Responsibilities.

Individual members of the board are required to:

1. Attend all board and committee meetings and functions, such as special events.

2. Stay informed about the organization's mission, services, policies and programs.

3. Review agenda and supporting materials prior to board and committee meetings.

4. Serve on committees or task forces and offer to take on special assignments.

5. Make a personal financial contribution to the organization.

6. Inform others about the organization.

7. Suggest possible nominees to the board who can make significant contributions to the work of the board and the organization.

8. Keep up-to-date on developments in the organization's field.

9. Follow conflict of interest and confidentiality policies.

10. Refrain from making special requests of the staff.

11. Assist the board in carrying out its fiduciary responsibilities, such as reviewing the organization's annual financial statements.

Chapter 8: Should I Be a Director?

In situations where you are a substantial shareholder in a company, it makes sense for you to be a director. What is substantial? In a small firm, anything over 10% would certainly be substantial. The owners and founders of a company usually comprise its first board of directors. It would be very unusual for a key person not to be a director.

If asked to be a director of a company, you have to weigh the pros and cons very carefully. You should first ask why you are being nominated. Is it because of your reputation or because of certain skills and contacts you may have? What potential risks and liabilities are you assuming by agreeing to serve on the board? To what extent can the company indemnify its directors against claims? What is your reward for taking such a risk? In this regard, stock option plans, or even better, stock purchase or ownership plans are very attractive inducements and can be very effective, especially in cases where one has been invited to serve on behalf of other shareholders without necessarily having a personal equity stake. Directors are often paid a fee in addition to any stock appreciation compensation they may have. Some companies pay a fixed amount per board meeting, others pay a monthly or annual retainer. A retainer, regardless of amount, is likely the best because, in principle, directorship is a full-time job.

A potentially problematic situation may occur if you are asked by a shareholder to serve on a board on that shareholder's behalf. For example, if you are an employee of a shareholder, i.e. where that shareholder is a corporate body, as may be the case in an investment company (e.g. a Venture Capital investor asks one of its investment managers to serve on an investee's board), you will be faced with a two-fold responsibility as well as exposing yourself personally, without necessarily being protected by the shareholder on whose behalf you are serving. Although liability insurance may reduce the potential liability, it will not eliminate it.

If you are asked to serve as a director for a company with which you or your employer have some other relationship with that company, e.g. a strategic alliance or vendor/supplier relationship, be extra cautious; you may find yourself in a conflict of interest situation by trying to serve two parties. When you agree to become a director of a company, you may be precluded from having any involvement with other companies due to non-competition or conflict of interest concerns. Because such restrictions may be imposed, not to mention the liability issues, directors must be appropriately compensated. Far too many people think they are doing a favour for a friend or business associate by serving as a director for them without any compensation. That's bad business for both parties.

Being asked to serve on a major corporate board such as Apple is a lot different than being asked to serve on the board of Fly-By-Night Enterprises. Many people view serving on high-profile prestigious boards as a valuable asset in their own career development not to mention the perks they might enjoy (such as free first-class air travel if they are on the board of an airline).

Being a director of a public company is an order of magnitude more onerous than being a director of a private company. In a private company, it is possible to learn about directors' responsibilities on-the-fly. This is not advisable for directors of public companies. Directors of public companies must familiarize themselves with the very extensive matters of corporate governance relating to the regulatory environment and the applicable securities legislation.

Are you a board member or just plain bored? Aside from everything else, being a board member should be fun and interesting. Don't join a board until you have met other board members. Consider a trial period i.e. date before you marry! Know something about the dynamics of the board first. Does the CEO listen to his board? Some board meetings can become exercises in showmanship or stress control while others are little more than fan clubs.

If you choose to accept a directorship, you will find that there are many resources available to you to help you become an effective director. There used to be no special qualification such as a certificate, diploma or belonging to a professional association in order to be a director. While this is still the case, some regulators do require or suggest that directors meet certain standards. We are likely to see more of this in the public arena.

Chapter 9: Questions About Boards.

1. What is a board of directors?

A corporation, whether for-profit or non-profit, is required to have a governing board of directors. A board of directors is made up of a group of senior advisors who oversee the activities of a company and represent its shareholders. Every public company must have a board of directors. Private companies are not required to have boards, although many of them do.

2. What is the difference between a for-profit "corporate" board and a non-profit board?

For-profit board members often are paid; non-profit board members usually are not. For-profit board members uniquely attend to decisions about dispersing profits to owners (shareholders) oftentimes in the form of stock equity and dividends. Non-profit board members do not seek to maximize and disperse profits to the owners; the owners of non-profits are members of the community. They serve in the interest of public stakeholders.

3. What does a board of directors do?

Corporate boards select, appoint, and review the performance of the chief executive and other key executives. They determine the direct compensation and incentive plan for these executives; ensure the availability of financial resources; review and approve annual budgets and company financials; and approve strategic decisions.

4. What is the role of the board's Chairman?

The Chairman of the board manages the board's business and acts as its facilitator and guide. Chairmen determine board composition and organization, clarify board and management responsibilities, plan and manage board committee meetings, and develop the effectiveness of the board. In many companies, CEOs serve as Chairman; in other companies the role is separated.

5. What is the difference between the CEO and the Chairman?

A CEO is a company's top decision maker; all other executives answer to him or her. CEOs are accountable to the board of directors for company performance. The Chairman of a company is the head of its board of directors. The board is elected by shareholders and is responsible for protecting investors' interests, such as the company's profitability and stability. The board selects the Chairman.

6. How many people are typically on corporate boards?

Boards typically have between 7 to 15 members, although some boards have as many as 31 members. The average board size is 10 members. Some analysts think boards should have at least seven members to satisfy the board roles and committees.

7. How do I find out how many women are on a company's board of directors?

Companies usually list their directors in the corporate governance section of their website. You can often identify the women by their names, but if not, you can go to the company's 10K document and read their bios.

8. What are corporate board committees?

There are four primary board committees; executive, audit, compensation, and nominating, although there may be others, depending on corporate philosophy and special circumstances relating to a company's line of business.

It's usually recommended that the compensation and audit committees be made up of independent directors. The executive committee is a smaller group that might meet when the full board is not available. The audit committee reviews the financial statements with internal auditors and outside audit companies. The compensation committee determines the salaries and bonuses of top executives, including the board itself. The nominating committee decides and nominate directors for the shareholders to vote their approval.

9. Why are some board members considered independent and others are not?

An independent director, or outside director, is a member of a board of directors who does not work for the company. Independent directors are important because they bring diverse backgrounds to decision making and are unbiased regarding company decisions. Independent directors are paid a standard fee for each board meeting. Inside directors are members of the corporation, usually part of the corporation's management team.

10. What are corporate bylaws and why are they important?

Corporate bylaws are rules that govern how a company operates. They state the rights and powers of shareholders, directors, and officers. If the board wishes to change bylaws, they often need to have shareholders vote for these changes.

11. What is conflict of interest?

Conflict of interest occurs when the personal or professional interests of a board member or senior executive are potentially at odds with the best interests of the corporation. Conflicts of interest often result in loss of public confidence and a damaged reputation. A conflict of interest might occur if two CEOs sit on each other's boards.

12. What are the qualifications to be on a corporate board of directors?

Individuals who are asked to serve on a board of directors have several years of executive experience or other equivalent professional experience in key areas that are beneficial to the company. Directors must be able to read, understand, and offer suggestions and comments on financial statements. Board members should be representative of the constituents that a company serves, including ethnic diversity, gender, and age.

13. How are new board members chosen?

In a public company, directors are selected based on criteria set by the nominating committee. Most new directors are chosen for their expertise in key areas that are useful to the corporation. Sometimes, CEOs and board chairs select directors they already know or, they will turn to executive search firms to find qualified candidates that meet their search criteria.

14. How has the role of the board of directors evolved over the years?

Many boards used to be comprised of employees, family members, and friends. But shareholder influence and government regulation now require boards to have independent directors not associated with the company or its executive team. Today there are many shareholder resolutions requiring companies to diversify their boards, and appoint directors of different backgrounds, gender, and race.

15. What is the time commitment of a board member?

Board directors must be able to commit the time necessary to responsibly fulfil their commitment to the organization. This includes board training, analyzing financial statements, reviewing board documents before board meetings, attending board meetings, serving on committees to which they are assigned, attending meetings, and doing whatever else the company requires. Most boards meet at least four times a year and some meet monthly.

16. What are the personal and professional benefits of being on a corporate board?

Being asked to serve on a corporate board is flattering. It shows that your skills are valued outside of your own organization. Directors meet interesting people and grapple with interesting issues. Independent director are often well paid.

17. How much do board members get paid?

Corporate directors are well compensated, and compensation is often determined by the size of the company. It's not unusual for corporate directors of large companies to be paid $100,000 or more each year they serve. They are often granted stock options, which could become very valuable.

18. Do boards have term or age limits?

Some boards have term limits and age limits and others do not. The National Association of Corporate Directors recommends term limits of 10 to 15 years to promote turnover and obtain fresh ideas. Age limits range from 70 to 80 years old, and many companies have no limit at all. Without term or age limits it is often difficult for companies to suggest to board members that they retire or leave.

19. How do boards of directors affect people and communities?

Boards of directors guide corporate behaviour. Decisions made by the boards of public companies can directly impact our daily lives. For example, a board might approve decisions to close or relocate factories or merge with other companies, which could result in loss of jobs in a community. Good companies often provide financial support to non-profit organizations in their communities.

20. Are boards required to consider diversity when electing directors?

There are no rules about board composition. But it is well recognized that diversity on boards contributes to better decision making. The Securities and Exchange Commission in the U.S adopted the ruling known as "The Governance Disclosure Rule" which requires companies to consider diversity when nominating director candidates. There is no standard, however, as to what constitutes a diverse board.

Chapter 10: Six Steps to Getting a Place on the Board.

You are a sitting chief executive officer who wants to see how another company's board governs. Or you are an aspiring CEO who wants to benefit from a valuable professional development opportunity and expand your marketability. Perhaps you are a newly retired executive who wants to stay active and connected. Or maybe you are a functional leader who wants to contribute your expertise in exchange for gaining a broader strategic perspective. You may even be a CEO or chief HR officer looking for ways to improve your own company's succession planning by getting your CEO-ready executives boardroom experience. Whether it is one of these or any other number of reasons, many of today's senior executives would like to join a corporate board of directors.

The irony is that while much has been written about the legitimate difficulties of companies finding qualified and interested directors for their boards, there are a growing number of prospective directors who would be all too happy to serve. If you are one of these prospective directors, the question is; how do you position yourself and navigate the nuances of the director selection process to get placed on a board.

Here are six steps to follow.

1. Board Bio: Create a compelling and concise board bio, which prominently outlines your skills and experiences. Focus on what you would bring to the boardroom. If you have financial expertise make that your key selling point. Many companies are wrestling with the impact of social media and are looking to bring that expertise into the boardroom. Others are seeking experience and relationships in China, India, Brazil and other emerging markets, so trumpet that if you have it. Of course, if you have experience interacting with a board of directors, highlight that as well. The key is to articulate the value that you will bring to another company's board.

2. Target List: Determine what types of boards would be most interesting and relevant for you. Serving as a director is a time consuming activity so you want to be enthusiastic about investing your time. What industry sectors or types of business issues are of greatest interest to you? Do you prefer private-equity backed or public companies? Make an expansive target list of companies whose boards would be of interest to you. Go through the Fortune 1,000 and Russell 2,000 and list the companies that would be of interest. Pay particular attention to lists of fastest growing companies and take a geographic cut. Think about private-equity (PE) or venture capital (VC) backed companies; be systematic and go through the websites of PE and VC firms and identify interesting portfolio companies and add them to your target list. Then organize the list into categories and identify the board members of each. You may be surprised to find people you know or one degree of separation away.

3. Your Interests: With board bio and target list in hand, you are now ready to get the word out. Express your interests to colleagues or people you know whom already serve on a board. These individuals are frequently approached about other board opportunities and might be too busy to pursue them and therefore able to refer you. Make other targeted outreaches to people who may be influential in director selection, including executive search firms that focus on director recruitment, lawyers, accountants, investment bankers, and management consultants. Be very focused in your "ask" for an introduction to a specific person or company or to be kept in mind should they be asked to recommend someone for a prospective director.

4. Director Events: Attend director education events, which offer the opportunity both to become more familiar with the governance issues confronting boards today, and meet well-connected individuals who can offer insights into the director selection process or recommend you at some point in the future. Expanding your own network through these types of events can be one of the most powerful ways to get into the community of board of directors.

5. Search Firms: Be responsive to outreach by the executive search firms that specialize in board director recruitment. Just remember that these firms represent the client company and are likely to only be able to place you on a board if your unique experience matches the criteria that they have been retained to find.

6. Not for Profits: Get started with a not-for-profit or community board. If you are eager to get going and corporate board opportunities have yet to materialize, it may be both pragmatic and fulfilling to pursue a directorship with an educational, healthcare, social services, or other mission-driven organization. Oftentimes these become stepping-stones for corporate boards through the interconnected web of relationships. If you are an excellent director, adding value and working collaboratively with others on your not-for-profit board, you may be surprised how directly this can create opportunities for other board directorships.

Board service is often a rewarding experience both professionally and personally. There is a growing demand for dedicated directors who can guide and govern our corporations. So if you want to be a board director and bring your expertise to bear, we offer these six steps to get you on your way.

Chapter 11: How to Get On a Corporate Board.

To get on a corporate board you must be qualified and be known. CEOs and board nominating committees look for board candidates with specific skill sets who are at the height of their careers. They also consider board dynamics, making sure that board members will work well together. For this reason, it's not unusual that CEOs and nominating chairs turn to people they know and trust to fill an open board seat. Qualified women are often less well known than their male counterparts, so they are not considered for selection. In some companies the criteria is so narrowly defined that few women qualify.

If you feel you are qualified to serve on a board or wish to join a board in the future, below are things you can do to advance your candidacy.

1. Expand your network.

A personal connection is one of the most important ways to facilitate a board position. Use your network to meet CEOs and senior executives in your field and let them know of your interest. Ask them to introduce you to other senior executives, board members, and professional recruiters. Participate in trade and professional associations and volunteer for the boards of non-profit and civic organizations.

2. Participate in a board training program.

Board training programs won't qualify you for board membership, but they can provide valuable information on how to position your candidacy. Curriculum topics include board readiness, networking tips, how to brand your skill sets, board governance, and how to read a financial report. Ask for references from past participants and inquire about how many past participants have been elected to a board seat.

3. Enhance your professional profile.

Become a self-promoter. Speak at professional meetings. Offer yourself as a subject matter expert to editors in the business and trade press. People who conduct board searches often look at newspapers and magazines to see who is being quoted and written about.

4. Start local.

Serving on the boards of non-profits, start-ups, industry, or trade associations is good training. These experiences will allow you to learn about board governance, strategic planning, marketing, finance, operations, and budgets. It is also a good way to get known as someone who can add value to a board.

Chapter 12: Steps to Becoming a Corporate Director.

Of all the career paths in business world, few can match the prestige and fascination of corporate board service. The honour of being selected to guide the future of an enterprise, combined with the intellectual challenge of helping that enterprise succeed despite the odds, make directorship a strong magnet for ambition and a worthy goal for accomplishment.

Furthermore, the pay can be decent. While directors do risk getting underpaid for the accordion-like hours they can be called upon to devote; (typical pay is a flat retainer plus stock, but hours are as needed with no upper limit), it's typically equivalent to CEO pay, if considered hour for hour. For example, a director can expect to work a good 250 hours for the CEO's 2,500 and to receive nearly 10 percent of the CEO's pay. In a public company that can provide marketable equity (typically half of pay), the sums can be significant low six figures for the largest global companies.

Granted, directorship cannot be a first career. As explained in other chapters of this book, boards offer only part time engagements and they typically seek candidates with track records. Yet directorship can be a fulfilling mid-career sideline, and a culminating vocation later in life for those who retire from day to day work, but still have much to offer.

So, at any age or stage, how can you get on a board? Here are 6 steps, representing common wisdom and some of my own insights based on what I have heard from directors who have searched for or who are seeking that first board seat.

1. Recast your resume and retune your mindset for board service. Before you begin your journey, remember that the most important readers of your resume will be board members in search of a colleague. As such, although they will be duly impressed by your skills and accomplishments as an executive, as they read your resume or talk to you in an interview they will be looking and listening for clues that you will be an effective director. Clearly, any board positions you have had including non-profit board service, work on special committees or task forces and the like should be prominent on your resume and in your mind.

2. Integrate the right keywords. Language can be tuned accordingly to "director-speak." Any language that suggests you singlehandedly brought about results should be avoided. Instead, use language about "working with peers," "dialogue," and "stewardship" or "fiduciary group decisions," "building consensus," and so forth. While terms such as "risk oversight," "assurance," "systems of reporting and compliance," and the like should not be overdone (boards are not politbureaus) they can add an aura of governance to an otherwise ordinary resume. This is not to suggest that you have two resumes; one for executive work and one for boards. Your use of board-speak can enhance an existing executive resume. So consider updating the resume you have on Bluesteps or any other executive search site and uploading that same resume to NACD's Directors Registry.

3. Suit up and show up. Make sure you attend your local chapter events and while you are there don't just shake hands, get to know people, talk to the speakers, and create opportunities for people to learn about you and your capabilities, not just your biography. Ensure when you are networking, that you are doing so with a purpose. Include in your conversations that you are ready, qualified, and looking for a board seat.

4. Cast a wide net. It is unrealistic for most candidates to aim for their first service to be on a major public company board. Your first board seat will likely be an unpaid position on a non-profit board, or an equity-only spot on a start-up private board, or a small-cap company in the U.S. or perhaps oversees. Consider joining a director association outside the U.S. Through the Global Network of Director Institutes' website you can familiarize yourself with the world's leading director associations. Some of them (for example, the Institute of Directors in New Zealand) send out regular announcements of open board seats, soliciting applications; The Institute of Directors in the United Kingdom (IoD) is a professional institute with members which promotes directors, develops corporate governance, represents its members. BlueSteps members also have access to board opportunities.

5. Join NACD. As long as you serve as a director on a board (including even a local non-profit) you can join NACD as an individual where you will be assigned your own personal concierge and receive an arrange of benefits far too numerous to list in this book.

6. Pace yourself. If you are seeking a public company board seat, bear in mind that a typical search time will be more than two years, according to a relevant survey from executive search firm. That is how long on average that both female and male directors responding to the survey said it took for them to get on a board once they started an active campaign. (A survey indicated that it took more time for women than men, but that discrepancy seems to have evened out now; good news considering studies by Credit Suisse and others showing a connection between gender diversity and corporate performance.) Remember that the two years is how long it took successful candidates to land a seat (people looking back from a boardroom seat on how long it took to get them there). If you average in the years spent by those who never get a board seat and gave up, the time would be longer. This can happen.

Chapter 13: Landing a Seat On a Corporate Board.

About 50 per cent of new board appointments are executives still in management roles. Another 40 per cent are executives who have retired from management. Ten per cent are people who have chosen a career shift out of management to become professional directors.

Here is what boards of directors are looking for.

1. Credentials
Someone who has held a C-level or managing partner title, or top executives in areas such as finance, law or human resources.

2. Experience
A track record volunteering on boards of associations or not-for profit organizations.

3. Certification
Directors' training or certification granted by the Institute of Corporate Directors.

4. Breadth
Executives who have worked across functions in an organization and have international experience.

5. Diversity
Female and visible-minority candidates, as boards seek to eliminate the impression they are "old boys' clubs."

6. Seasoning
A solid track record; at least 10 years in senior management. Experience with turnarounds and reinvention.

7. Staying Current
Up-to-date knowledge of financial rules, governance standards and technology.

8. Time
Sufficient time to read relevant material and prepare for monthly or quarterly meetings and do the committee work that follows.

9. Making them love you.
Corporate leaders are more likely to win board appointments at other firms if they employ subtle and sophisticated forms of flattery and demonstrations of conformity with other board members.

To tap into the corporate elite's inner circle, a person cannot be too obvious. Being too overt with one's intentions can be interpreted as manipulative or political and ruin chances of joining a board.

Based on interviews with corporate directors and chief executive officers of large U.S. and U.K. industrial and service firms, they identified tactics in selection interviews that are most likely to make directors believe a candidate is on their wavelength and win them a seat at the board table.

a. Flattery as advice seeking: Congratulate an influential member about a recent success. "How were you able to close that deal so successfully?"

b. Arguing, then agreeing: "At first, I didn't see your point but it makes total sense now. You have convinced me."

c. Side-stream compliments: Praise an influential board member to his or her friends, hoping word gets back to them.

d. Get on a wavelength: "I am the same way. I am with you 100 per cent."

e. Conform to opinions: Covertly learn of chairman's opinions from his/her contacts, and then conform with their opinions in conversations with others who can influence the decision.

f. Point out connections: Reference religious or political connections the individuals have in common.

Chapter 14: What It Takes to Get On Board.

It's neither as simple nor as difficult as people may think. Following this practical advice can increase your chances of being able to serve on a board.

There are three popular myths about getting on a board.

Myth Number 1: Because of the shortage of directors willing to serve, it's easy to get on a board today.

Reality: Most active chief executive officers now limit their outside board seats to one, and even retired executives seldom serve on more than three or four. Directors are being more selective about the board invitations they accept, and some highly qualified executives refuse to consider serving at all. Board invitations are, indeed, rolling in for experienced directors. But landing your first board seat is still no easy matter.

Myth Number. 2: The best way to get a board seat is to send your CV to a search firm.

Reality: Search firms are retained to find directors to serve on boards, not to find board seats for potential directors. While some do add unsolicited CVs to their databanks, others simply ignore them. Meeting with a recruiter to express interest in board service seldom yields results either. If the stars align such that you happen to meet when he/she is conducting a search where your background is a fit, your name may be put forward. But many who take this approach wait by the phone in vain.

Myth Number. 3: Serving on a not-for-profit board will get you on a for-profit board.

Reality: Only if someone on that board serves on a for-profit board that is looking for a new director and puts your name forward. Most search-firm databases focus on directors serving on public company boards, in part because many of the databases are comprised of information gleaned from proxy circulars. Serving on a not-for-profit board can give you a taste of whether you enjoy being a board member. It can also provide references from fellow trustees that are often useful when you are being considered for a for-profit board. But it is by no means a straight shot from the not-for-profit boardroom to the Standard & Poor's 1500.

So, if you have never served on the board of a public company, how do you go about getting on one?

1. Your own board may be your best resource.

While some boards refuse to allow their chief executives to accept another board seat, the more enlightened ones recognize the benefits of having their CEO serve elsewhere. If your board is supportive, your directors may be your best resource in finding another board to serve on. Senior executives approaching retirement, such as a chief financial officer or leader of a major business unit, may also be able to provide leads. Letting directors with whom you have worked know of your interest in taking on a board seat post-retirement may be the easiest way for you to find one.

If you are a new CEO or recently appointed president/chief operating officer with some assurance that the corner office lies ahead, serving on another board can be an important step in your professional development, helping you understand how better to work with your own board.

2. Tap into Director Registries.

Nasdaq recently launched a new registry of prospective directors. The Web site creates a profile through a series of questions that can then be retrieved by boards searching for new directors. The National Association of Corporate Directors offers a similar director registry the U.S..

3. For prospective directors who offer diversity, three other associations may be able to help.

Catalyst keeps a database on women executives. The Executive Leadership Council helps to provide board opportunities for African-American executives. The Hispanic Association on Corporate Responsibility serves as a resource for Hispanic executives interested in board service.

4. Target and Network.

Consider the type of board where your experience would have greatest relevance and develop a list of target companies where your background might be a particular asset. Then pull up bios of their current board members. Do they have directors who already bring the skills you offer? Are any approaching retirement? Do you know anyone on that board or someone who is likely to know one of the directors through business, social or political contacts?

Many directors have found their first board seat through other networks involving auditors, executive compensation consultants, or lawyers they have worked with who service several board clients. Others have landed their first seat by expressing interest to contacts in venture capital firms who might become involved in initial public offerings.

Getting that first board seat remains a challenge, even for highly qualified business leaders. But once you land your first, more board invitations will follow.

Chapter 15: Joining Boards: It's Not Just Who You Know That Matters.

For many, a corporate directorship is a career capstone. But attaining one is far from easy. No one can say for sure how to get on a corporate board, but many people point to two routes; the first is to break into the "right" network and the second is to seek a progression of board seats that begins with, for example, a seat on a not-for-profit or community board and eventually results in appointment to a corporate board.

Both paths are problematic; neither is particularly transparent or relies on objective measures and given that many boards are stubborn bastions of white masculinity, pursuing the "right" network can be fraught, especially for women and other diverse candidates. Indeed, our research reinforces that concern; many boards still rely on their own (mostly white, mostly male) networks to fill seats.

There's a different way; one that is more measurable, controllable and offers greater transparency. It starts with a focus on skills. Although many boards continue to select new members from their own networks, our research suggests that more are beginning to implement objective processes to select members based on the skills and attributes that boards need to be effective. A survey of more than 1,000 corporate directors across the globe, found that

48% of the boards had a formal process of determining the combination of skills and attributes required for their board and, therefore, for new directors.

We know this approach can work because we have seen it: We studied a large corporation that was being split into two public companies for which two new boards had to be created. The chairman wanted to create two balanced boards, with the mix of skills, knowledge, and experience each company needed. He appointed a special team to create an objective, transparent method for selecting the directors. After reviewing the roles and responsibilities of each board and the natures of the new businesses, the team derived lists of the skills each board needed. Then it created a model containing the dimensions critical to a high-performing board, from functional and industry expertise to behavioural attributes. This approach led both companies to recruit board members that were diverse in needed strategic skills. Both boards are on to a good start, demonstrating that when a firm builds a board using a rigorous assessment of the qualities it needs to carry out its governance task, rather than personal networks, the board is better equipped to execute its functions.

In our survey, we also asked about specific skills. We wanted to know which were the strongest skills represented on boards and which were missing. Directors named industry knowledge, strategy, and financial-audit expertise as their strongest skill sets and 43% cited technology expertise, HR-talent management, international-global expertise, and succession planning as the skills missing most on their boards.

We also looked at results by industry and region. The industry with the greatest skills gap was IT and telecommunications, whose boards are in serious need of international-global expertise and HR-talent management.

The region with the greatest board-level skills gap is Asia, where risk management and merger and acquisition adeptness are sorely needed.

Based on our research and experience with boards, we believe that the future of director selection is becoming an increasingly objective and skill-focused process. Networks aren't going away, but aspiring directors may want to approach their search by asking not only, "what skills do I need to get on a board?," but also by looking at what skills boards already possess and what skills boards need. One strategy might be investing in your own human capital to become the board member corporations need.

Chapter 16: Women in the Boardroom.

Many professional women (and men) do not consider board positions as a viable adjunct to a successful career. Board positions are often regarded as being for retiring c-suite executives, business leaders and partners in law and accounting firms or voluntary positions on charities for well connected people with time on their hands and aged over 50.

In the modern world of improving corporate governance this perception is being challenged. Board positions are increasingly being taken by working executives, younger people and women. This is particularly the case in countries with quotas and those with strong regulatory systems or mandated corporate governance guidelines for public listed companies, such as the UK.

The renewed focus on corporate governance arising from the global financial crisis has resulted in a growing awareness across all sectors in the UK of the benefits that diversity and gender balance bring to the boardroom. The question that arises for many women is how to get there?

Below are some tips from Women on Boards for anyone thinking about board positions now, or in the future.

1. Consider your motivations for being a board member.

Directors govern an organisation on behalf of owners, shareholders and stakeholders so you need to be comfortable in your role as a fiduciary (an individual who acts in the interest of another person or an organisation). To join a board, in particular a charity board, it is helpful to have an affiliation with the sector in which the organisation operates, an interest in its purpose and be able to commit the appropriate time to be a valuable board member.

2. Know your company's policy about employees taking board roles.

Are you allowed to go on boards and if so, which ones, and what is the approval process? If there is not a formal process then ask Human Resource to develop one and offer you assistance.

3. Consider the sector you are most interested in and best suited to.

Understand how the skills you have used in your career can be adapted to board roles; this is commonly called your transferable skill set. It includes the assets you have gained through experience, rather than your pure technical skill set.

Once you have a clear understanding of your transferable skills, consider sectors and types of organisations they might best suit. Think laterally; you might be surprised how much a hospital is like an airline.

4. Let others know of your board ambitions.

Ask yourself "how many people know of my board aspirations?" If the number is low or zero, there is work to be done. In many sectors there are more candidates than roles so it can be a competitive process.

Appointments are still often made on the basis of recommendation. It is human nature to favour people we know or people who are recommended by people we know. Of all sectors, government appointments tend to have the most transparent processes.

5. Be financially literate and understand directors' duties.

If you are not comfortable with standard sets of accounts and aware of the liabilities and responsibilities of a director, then do something about it. There are a range of courses and programs you can do online or face to face.

6. Consider what value you add to a board.

You need to be clear about the value you bring to a board. Match your skill set to the needs identified (or not) by the board. Sometimes you might be a great candidate but the timing is wrong. Rather than beat yourself up that you did not get the role, just move on and look for another one. Serendipity does play a part.

7. Have a good board ready CV and a professional pitch.

Some experts says that your board CV is not your professional career CV. It should be concise (not more than two pages) and contain a summary of your transferable and profession skills (not your role) and the value you bring.

Key words around competence and areas of speciality are important. The colloquial version of your summary is your pitch. Use it when introducing yourself at networking functions and when you bump into someone who can help you.

Part of your pitch is being ready to do "the ask" when you line up coffee meetings with influential people who can help you; they will not expect their time to be wasted with idle chit chat.

8. Start to think like a director.
There is an old saying; "if you waddle like a duck, swim like a duck and act like a duck ... then you are a duck.". To become a successful director you need not only to fit the part, but look and act the part. Remember, a board member sits above an organisation and does not work in it, so your language and positioning needs to reflect a more elevated role where wisdom and judgement are more valued than organisational capacity to get the job done.

Chapter 17: Why Women Over 50 Should Join Non-profit Boards.

Serving on the board of a non-profit is a wonderful, enriching experience, especially for women who are in their 50s or older. Aside from the joy of working for the public good, it can broaden your resume and skills, which might help you find your next job, especially if you want to transition from the corporate world into the non-profit field.

In exchange for all this, you will need to commit some time and probably money. Depending on the non-profit, you may have to attend meetings more or less monthly, raise money, help plan and run events and improve the group's programming. Unlike corporate boards, a non-profit typically won't pay you for your efforts. Most likely you will be expected to donate a tax-deductible donation to the non-profit periodically.

Here are some tips.

1. Determine which causes are meaningful to you and be ready to provide proof of your passion when you are interviewed for a board position. Can you sincerely show that you have a passionate interest in a certain non-profit's mission and care genuinely about the challenges and pressing issues on its agenda?

If so, you are on the right track. But you are not a shoe-in. You will be interviewed and vetted by the board, so you will need to prepare for what is essentially a job interview. Your passion and commitment for the organization and cause is what will set you apart from other candidates.

2. Zero in on what you have to offer. Boards are often looking for people who can help them in specific areas, like fundraising, PR and marketing, event planning and finances. If you have any of those skills, play them up.

Moreover, your time, energy, intelligence and financial resources or connections are worth something.

3. Think strategically about what being on the non-profit's board can do for you. Use the board to build your knowledge of a particular mission area and a specific skill set, but also as a platform to show your expertise and competence to influential people in the non-profit and for-profit world.

If you plan to leverage your position to land a job in the non-profit sector or an entrepreneurial venture with social purpose, consider the connections you can make through the board you are aiming to join.

One way to do this is to ask the board's leader to tell you about its other members. Most people who sit on non-profit boards are also sitting on others or have sat on others in the past. Consequently, they know people in lots of other organizations and may be able to steer you to dozens of non-profit decision makers.

4. See if you are impressed by the way the board has run the non-profit. Ask for written board policies, bylaws and previous minutes. Then invite current and former board members for coffee, to find out what their experience has been like.

You should also check out the organization's latest online tax filing to see how much its key employees and executives earn. This will give you a sense of where the money goes and whether the pay is out of sync with the group's operating budget.

5. Understand why the board wants you and what it wants out of you. Is it for your skills? Your access to potential donors? Your own giving power?

To learn what's specifically expected of you, nail down answers to the following questions.
1. How much time will I be asked to give?
2. When does the board work get done?
3. Are the meetings on weekends, weeknights or weekdays?
4. How long will I need to serve?
5. How big a donation will I have to make to the group, and how often?
6. Will I have to use my connections to raise funds?

Local Boards vs. National Boards

One more question to ask yourself is whether you did rather devote your energy to a local non-profit or a national one.

A local board may give you a better chance to be involved at the ground level, but it can be a time bandit if you are not careful. Serving on a national board can be a little headier; its members may be key players in their respective industries, and the organization is more likely to have a high-profile, high-impact mission.

Whichever boards you end-up; I hope you help bring increased awareness to their causes and make a difference in others' lives.

Chapter 18: How to Find a Rewarding Non-profit Board Position.

Becoming a member of a non-profit organization's board can be a meaningful way to explore how an individual's experience and expertise can be applied in the non-profit sector at the governance level, and ultimately, how one's experience and expertise can help advance a non-profit organization's social impact. It also can be a rewarding, high impact way that for-profit executives can do community service while learning new skills that can enhance their own careers.

When you join a board, what you are really saying is that you agree to put your personal interests and ambitions in the background and you are there to best serve the best interests of that organization.

With serving the best interests of an organization in mind, it's important to choose social causes you are most passionate about. I believe the single most important element in being a successful board member and helping to make a board much more effective is your own interest and passion in the work of that group. On a board, and a non-profit board in particular, you are meant to be an ambassador. If you, as an ambassador, don't feel passionate about the work of this organization, who will?

To explore your passion for a particular cause, it can help to walk through a series of questions.

1. Is the work of the organization interesting to me?
2. Could I imagine making the organization one of my leading philanthropies, in terms of the time, energy, and other personal resources I am willing to devote to it?
3. How willing would I be to introduce others to the work of the organization?

It also can help to volunteer with an organization. Many organizations have fundraising events staffed by volunteer committees, such as "Friends of the Board." Helping out at one of these events or joining an event committee can provide opportunities to learn more about the organization, its mission, and its board, and in turn, help you better explore your passion for its work.

Determining which opportunities are best.

After you have determined those causes you are truly passionate about, you can begin to evaluate specific opportunities. Four fundamental questions can help you determine whether a particular position will be the right fit.

1. Are my goals the same as those of this organization and its board?
2. Can I contribute skills, experience, or expertise that will increase the impact of the organization and help it advance its mission?

3. Am I prepared to commit the time required to fulfil my legal and fiduciary responsibilities as a board member?
4. Am I required to give/raise money for this board and can/will I do that?

1. Are my goals the same as those of this organization and its board?

Finding out who else is on the board can offer a sense of whether or not you are likely to fit into that group. Discover what interests they represent, their goals as individual members and as a group, and how they work together. Also determine what kind of relationship the board has with the executive directors. Does the executive directors consider the board an asset to the organization? Do the executive directors and the board chair work together to find ways to engage the skills of each board member? If your goal in joining a board is to learn and use your skills to have a positive impact on the organization and its mission, then it would be extremely frustrating to find yourself on a body that was effectively a rubber stamp for management. You have got to really match the way this board functions to your values system. You have to make sure there is a fit.

When I look at a new board opportunity; I look for signs that there is a strong, committed leader at the helm who engages the board in decision-making at the organization. Good leaders make board members feel good about what they are doing. I imagine board involvement is not going to be much fun or successful if the leaders aren't strong. I once resigned from one board that did not meet my expectations. They had only one meeting a year where they did get everyone together to eat lobster. They were just using board members' names for their letterhead. There wasn't a meaningful engagement.

2. Can I contribute skills, experience, or expertise that will increase the impact of the organization and help it advance its mission?

People considering joining a board should evaluate their ability to have impact and to help advance the mission of the organization. People who love board service are those who become meaningfully engaged. In addition to fulfilling their fiduciary obligations as board members, they bring a needed professional skill, relevant experience, or subject matter knowledge to the board room. Evaluate barriers that might get in the way of making such a contribution and whether they can be overcome. For example, if you are being recruited by a non-profit that the board wants to scale because you have built several businesses, make sure that the CEO has the capabilities to grow the organization or is coachable. If the organization wants to mount a public relations (PR) campaign and you are the PR executive they are bringing on the board to help, make sure that there is a staff that can execute your ideas or be prepared to row a labouring.

Clues to how effective a non-profit board is; can be found by reviewing its bylaws, its meeting schedule, its budget, its use of external auditors, and the minutes of prior board meetings (although some minutes may be confidential). I would recommend asking about the rotation schedule for seats on the board and committee chair assignments. You don't want to see people in lifetime jobs. Other information that could be instructive is whether the current board members enjoy serving on the board and whether there is a waiting list of people hoping to join.

The other side to making sure the board's goals fit with yours is to determine whether your skills meet the board's needs. Many boards have informal (or formal) limits on the number of members within specific professional specialties, i.e., one human resources expert slot, one academic slot, one legal expert slot, etc. But even if you are a lawyer and the board you are interested in already has several lawyers; you should think about what unique skills you may bring to the table that can boost the organization's social impact.

It's a question of analyzing the skill sets they have and then the board itself being very clear about what it is about you that they would find interesting or you identifying that yourself. What is the unique skill set I would bring that could serve this board?"

Directors who are currently most in demand in the non-profit sector are those who can bring financial acumen to the table, regardless of their professional specialty. One of the primary responsibilities of a non-profit board member is financial oversight that is extremely difficult to do if you don't know the difference between an income statement and a balance sheet.

3. Am I prepared to commit the time required to fulfil my oversight responsibilities and prepared to take on the legal and fiduciary responsibilities of being a board member?

People familiar with non-profit board service said that those who are new to the sector often underestimate the amount of time required to be an effective board member. In fact, the time commitment for many non-profit boards can be substantial. Non-profit boards have many legal and fiduciary responsibilities, established by law. It is vital that board members become informed about those responsibilities and the role that they will play as an individual and a group to fulfil them.

Quarterly meetings are the norm in the U.S and monthly meeting are the norm in the UK, with each meeting lasting up to three-quarters of a day and requiring a few hours of preparation time in advance. In addition, many board members go through a multi-day orientation program at the beginning of their tenure and are required to participate on one or more subcommittees. For a mid-sized, average board, it's not unrealistic that you could expect people to be committing 75 to 100 hours per year.

Not that long ago, the whole idea of board service was the opportunity to mix with some of your peers. It was a collegial kind of thing; it was fun to do. But the requirements weren't terribly onerous. What we have seen is a steady ramping up of requirements and responsibilities of sitting on a board. So, it's not to be entered into lightly.

In addition to asking how much time your service on a particular board will take, you might ask questions about how that time will be spent. For example, are the board meetings strategic? Do meetings focus on issues that matter the most? Is the chair of the board a committed and skilled leader? Are board members well informed about their roles and responsibilities? "High-performing boards have high-performing chairs that manage the agenda and group dynamics in a way that enables board members to contribute their full intellectual capital to the organization. If the board in question is not performing at this level, be prepared to be patient, or step up to leadership yourself.

I spends as much as 15 percent of my time doing work for the various non-profit and for-profit boards and commissions on which I serves, but I felt that my efforts make a difference within the organizations and to society as a whole. I take it "board service" seriously. I try to put in a huge amount of time. You really have to believe passionately in the organization's mission. It is hard work. It ebbs and flows, but it's hours and hours. You have to really get involved. You have got to be at the meetings. They really need you there.

4. Am I required to give/raise money for this board and can/will I do that?

Not all nonprofits require board members to raise money; some rely on government funding or generate earned income streams; however, many non-profits rely on donations from others, and those non-profit boards ask members to either donate or raise a specific amount of money for the organization. The amounts can vary widely throughout the sector and sometimes even within the same board. Non-profit boards typically require some combination of these three things from board members; time, talent, and treasure. If a board member has particular skills and/or is willing to commit substantial time to the organization, he or she may not be asked to participate as much in fundraising as other members; however, that in tough economic times, all board members may be asked to step up their level of giving.

In non-profit board I served in the past; they usually expected to provide more expertise than cash; however, I invested in the success of the organizations on whose boards I serves that I oftentimes gets swept up by the generosity of other board members and makes a financial commitment, as well. Board giving can motivate even the poorest members of the board to give.

The key is to know what the financial expectations are up front and to decide whether you are able to meet those expectations. If you are not prepared to get involved in fundraising and the expectation is that you are going to raise money, that is going to be frustrating all around. In short, do you have the resources and is the organization's mission important enough to you that you are willing to commit not only some of your own financial resources, but to encourage other people you know to commit theirs, too?

For non-profit executives, serving on a non-profit board can enhance career development by providing a different perspective on what it takes at the governance level to deliver impact, raise resources, and ensure accountability. For executives moving into the non-profit sector for the first time, finding the right non-profit board role can be very rewarding. Dedicated, effective for-profit executives can leverage their experience and professional expertise to boost the social impact of the organization. At the same time, the executives can gain new skills and knowledge about non-profits that could help them consider careers in the sector. It's a wonderful way to learn at the same time as giving something back. Most of the time, you are forced into one or the other of those roles. It's not very often in life that you get that opportunity to do both.

Chapter 19: Essential Elements of Board-Building.

Boards are being criticized even as they are being given more responsibilities than ever. There is much criticism aimed at boards of directors these days, and justifiably so in many cases. Boards of many well-respected, important companies have fallen short in the area of governance. Indeed, there are directors who have gone public about the shortcomings of their respective boards. It's one thing to acknowledge that mistakes have been made; it's quite another to overhaul a board in a meaningful way and take it to a higher level of performance. In the past 12 years I have worked with dozens of boards and haven't found one that could not raise its game significantly. If you are serious about making your board more effective and actually getting significant value from it, there are five essential elements that need to be addressed.

1. Composition

Perhaps the most obvious component of board-building is composition; ensuring that the portfolio of skills resident at the board table is optimal in terms of the company's business model and strategic direction. Effective board composition goes beyond skill sets; board members are only effective if they are engaged. Nothing is worse than a highly qualified director "on paper" who really isn't contributing much in board discussions. Making sure that directors are not "over-boarded" and can devote the share of mind required to be effective is an integral component of reviewing board composition. Conducting an individual director peer review; where a third party collects confidential feedback from other board members on an individual director's performance can also be a helpful exercise.

2. Information

The quality of board discussion and decision-making is directly related to the quality of information the board receives. Management is often accused either of providing sparse data or, as is more common, so much that board members have to wade through an inordinate amount of information before reaching the "aha" moment.

Boards typically receive an avalanche of financial data but a woeful lack of information on competitors, industry trends, and other factors relative to the context of business operations. Directors often complain privately about the information they receive and how it is presented but rarely ask the CEO and management for changes. If your board has not talked about board pre-reading materials, make it a topic for an upcoming executive session.

3. Leadership

The debate over the separation of the chairman and CEO roles continues. Yet regardless of what a board does about its leadership structure, it's important not to lose sight of the real issue; leadership effectiveness. Does the person running the meetings such as board meetings, committee meetings, or executive sessions provide effective leadership? Does the person draw out different perspectives, manage the board's time well, and drive to consensus on key issues? Do the leaders of the board have a constructive not a cosy or a hostile working relationship with the CEO and other top executives? Are they respected by the other board members and the management team? Absent the title, would they be the natural, informal leader of the group? Do other board members and management engage them outside of the boardroom on issues of concern and value their perspectives?

4. Dynamics

Many directors view this as the single most important factor in board effectiveness. This is, essentially, how the board works together as a team and works with the CEO and senior management. Is the climate of the boardroom open, energized, and positive? Or is it guarded, polarized even hostile? Or are board meetings tiresome, with attention flagging and directors constantly checking their watches?

You can put in place all of the governance "best practices" you can find but none of them will have much impact if the board lacks an engaged and energized dynamic.

5. Key Responsibilities

Given the amount of debate being generated over executive pay, one might begin to think that a board's single most important responsibility is determining the compensation of the CEO. While that is not unimportant, it receives an inordinate amount of attention because it's the one area where proxy disclosure has enabled outsiders to gain some insight into the board's decision-making processes.

What is seldom heard about and what typically matters more with regard to shareholder value is how the board engages on issues of corporate strategy, CEO and executive succession planning, and risk oversight.

Frankly, most boards have not been doing a very good job in any of these three areas, as evidenced by a survey of more than 600 public company board members. Less than 15% of those surveyed rated their board as "highly effective" on strategic planning and oversight; 30% rated their board as only "somewhat effective" or "below acceptable levels" in this area. It was even worse on CEO succession, with less than 12% rating their board as "highly effective" in this critical area and more than 50% rating their board only "somewhat effective" or "below acceptable levels." Risk oversight barely got above 10% in terms of "highly effective" ratings; nearly 35% of directors ranked their board only "somewhat effective" or "below acceptable levels."

There are no quick fixes on this list. Yet attention to these issue can truly make boards more effective. Identifying and beginning to address even two or three areas to work on can have a notable impact on any board.

Chapter 20: Board Effectiveness.

The definition of board effectiveness has shifted dramatically over the past decade. In the aftermath of the global financial crisis and numerous corporate scandals, a director now confronts not only complex oversight accountability, but also personal risk and liability. Clearly, this is a job not for the faint of heart.

As the supply of courageous board candidates dwindles, global companies are in need of battle-tested directors more than ever; board members who fully understand and can actively engage in virtually all aspects of an enterprise's operations. To be truly effective, a board needs directors who can work as a group to clearly define their role and mission, and in specialized individual roles, such as succession planning, acquisitions and capital allocation.

In this context, it's become rather easy today to identify the weakest boards. Typically, such boards comprise directors who act distant and detached; traits anathema to a business environment that demands transparency and accountability.

My colleagues and I recently studied what makes some boards more effective than others. We found that boards tend to progress from good-to-great along a four-phase continuum.
1. Foundational
2. Developed
3. Advanced
4. Strategic.

Essential to creating a high-performance board is agreement and alignment, at the outset, on where the board actually stands in this continuum and where it needs to be.

The continuum essentially represents a corporate hierarchy of needs, akin to the famous personal-development hierarchy created by psychologist Abraham Maslow. In the corporate model, you equate a "foundational board," which provides basic compliance oversight, to basic survival needs such as food and shelter in the human hierarchy. Similarly, a "strategic board," which provides prescient forward-looking insights to form a company's foundational strategy, is fully actualized and high-performing.

Foundational survival boards focus on compliance; they play it safe. These are the weak performers in the corporate food chain, with directors who are unwilling to take strong positions, make tough decisions, or play proactive operational roles.

Strategic actualized, in Maslow's terms boards underpin high-performance companies, where directors take appropriate risk to make significant contributions and lasting impact on enterprise value.

So how can weak boards advance along the effectiveness continuum if they find themselves clinging to survival basics? In our study, we found five elements; "disrupters" that tend to hinder the progression of boards toward self-actualization and high performance.

1. Lack of clarity on the roles of individual directors and the board as a whole. Role ambiguity slows decision-making and causes unnecessary director conflicts.

2. Poor process management hinders effective board preparation, meeting management, and communications. This results in indecisiveness and a lack of urgency on critical challenges facing the organization.

3. Lack of alignment and agreement on company strategy causes disinterest among board members, who then simply default to tackling regulatory and compliance issues. Poor strategic alignment also hampers a board's ability to prioritize issues and set their near-term agendas. This often causes board disruption and sends damaging signals to financial markets.

3. Poor team dynamics fracture boards and lead to power struggles. Like any effective working group, a board should be comprised of professional peers who respect and work well with each other.

4. Board composition is a serious impediment, if not done right. Today's challenges require new perspectives and skills. But boards often lack the ability to objectively evaluate their makeup to determine if they have the right people and skills at the table.

I have seen my fair share of effective boards and dysfunctional ones. The worst cases nearly always exhibit at least one of the disruptors described above.

Classic dysfunctional examples include organizations where the company founder dominates board discussions and stifles all attempts to change and modernize the company or alter the composition of the board (i.e., poor team dynamics). In other cases, highly compensated boards literally run a company into the ground by churning through CEO after CEO (lack of strategic alignment). Other weak-performing boards focus on recruiting "big-name" directors; typically high-profile CEOs who are simply too distracted by operational and financial issues facing their own companies to make any significant contribution (poor board composition).

In stark contrast, I have worked with board chairs who had the foresight and courage to spin off a successful division to help that now-standalone unit focus its resources on building its brand and market presence. In these instances, short-term personal gains were cast aside in favour of the long-term viability and health of the division and the corporate entity.

The board of an international restaurant chain, for instance, played a leading role in reducing the company's overall risk profile. Specifically, a director personally spearheaded the development and adoption of an advanced enterprise resource planning system, working hand-in-hand with internal staff. Another high-performing board immersed itself into a global financial services firm's complex financing activities, as it successfully navigated a financial crisis. These directors went well beyond basic compliance to provide true strategic counsel.

To add such strategic value, high-performing boards must be "talent-centric." At its most basic level, this manifests itself in a board's composition and diversity level. An enterprise must attract directors who can provide valuable, strategic input, while building a board that can draw on the diversity of its members' expertise and backgrounds across geographies, gender, race, and experience to create a whole that is literally greater than the sum of its parts.

Strategic directors also commit to performing at their full potential and have the courage and self-confidence to raise and address any personal developmental needs. They also must be able to give constructive feedback to other directors to enhance the personal effectiveness of their board colleagues. A number of talent-development tools are available to help, including individual director and board assessments that gauge learning agility (the ability to learn from past experience and manage amid uncertainty) and other valuable traits and skills.

Effective corporate governance is more complex and challenging than ever. Companies need boards to help them meet regulatory compliance basics. But the most effective boards are those that easily check that box, while also delivering solid strategic counsel and direction. Recruiting and developing directors who go well beyond basic needs is the secret to building a high-performing, fully actualized board.

Chapter 21: Building a High Performing Fully Actualized Board.

Building an A class board of directors generates a serious multiplier effect for your organization. Yet, few people properly build their boards. Instead of selecting powerful action oriented advocates and champions many founders and CEOs gather a collection of name plates which produce marginal results.

If you are going to build a board, select lions over cats.

The Cats.

Name plates, talkers and playful companions do not make effective board members. Yes, they might have money, connections and a proven track record, yet you must ask yourself if they are going to truly direct their powers to help you as the founder and chief executive to achieve your greatest impact and have your organization reach its peak performance.

If the board members are inactive or producing marginal results, then what you have done is put cat in place of where you need lions and while the DNA heritage might be the same, the scope, scale and reach of their hunting skills differ dramatically.

The Lions

Lions are individuals who produce serious results. They understand that it is a privilege to serve in this role and that it takes an enduring commitment to materialize a vision. They are in it to leverage their know-how, know-who and honest opinion towards the organization.

They measure their impact in terms of exponential results. They hunt clients, contributors, enabling partners and A class talent on behalf of the organization. Exceptional board members continuously cultivate and help build the leadership skills of the founder and c-level executives. Below are some of the talents of a Lion.

1. Finding clients and contributors.

A business or social venture lives or dies on clients or contributors. A lion board member will use his or her apex hunting skills to help track down and secure additional market opportunities and potential donors. Note, if a board member is resistant to helping, you must ask yourself if it is you or your organization's performance to date. You must be a peak performer in order to merit their support.

2. Enabling Partners plus A class talents.

Building partnerships and alliances are key to any firm's or social venture's development. It is essential to search, select and approach the best partners at each stage of growth. Also, as founders and chief executives develop their firms, they must expand their management team. They must bring on the best and brightest to drive the firm from growth point to growth point. Lion talented board of directors open up their know-how and leverage them towards the organization.

3. Cultivate the Leadership Team.

The ultimate testimony of an effective board member is a willingness to continuously cultivate the talent of the chief executive, founder and leadership team. They push, drive, inquire and encourage the leader to develop their skills, know-how and leadership skills. Their goal is to help management grow into full A Class apex leaders. For the lion level board member, the ultimate sign of success is the ability of the leadership team to reach exponential and sustained growth.

Finding this calibre board member takes time and effort and if you want lion level individuals as board members, then you must be willing to work incredibly hard across difficult terrain and prove day in and day out that you merit their hard earned wisdom.

Chapter 22: Barriers to Board Effectiveness in Non-profit Organisation.

There are a number of factors that help to explain why some boards don't function effectively. Taken together, the factors below provides a checklist for assessing a board and identifying problem areas. Examining these barriers to board effectiveness can be the first step in revitalizing an existing board or building from scratch. Let's take a look at some of the factors now.

1. Temptation to micro-management. Practically everyone can share hair-raising stories about boards that spent untold hours discussing trivial subjects while neglecting major agenda items deserving their more careful deliberation. It is critical that the board focuses its attention on items of critical importance to the organization. In order to do this, the board must avoid the temptation to micro-manage or meddle in lesser matters or in areas that are more appropriately handled by the professional staff. The average board, meeting monthly for two hours, has approximately 24 hours of meeting time per year to make all of the major decisions as well as address critical issues that come before it unannounced. It is simply impossible to do an effective job with-in those 24 hours of meeting time, even if only a few hours are wasted on trivia.

2. Ineffective Nominating Committee. Many boards lack an effective nominating committee. We need to remember that the work of the nominating committee has lasting impact on organization and this committee's work determines who board leaders will be for many years for years into the future. The nominating committee should be well organized, have a clear sense of recruiting priorities as well as expectations for individual board members especially in the area of fund-raising. These elements are frequently missing in many organizations. If the nominating committee or board recruiting committee is poorly organized, board members in turn are not likely to have a good understanding of the organization and their role as board members.

3. No Plan for Rotation. Another problem is the lack of a plan for orderly rotation of board members on and off the board. If the same people serve year after year, there is no way for new blood and new ideas to come into the board. Despite their sense of commitment, these same people will make the organization a "closed corporation." Rotation prevents the ingrown possessiveness sometimes found on self-perpetuating boards. In a time of rapid change, the presence of new people who bring a new perspective will promote creativity and innovation in board decision-making.

4. Failure to remove unproductive members. Another problem that leads to poor performance is the failure to remove unproductive board members. People who are not carrying out their commitments as board members become major blocks to overall board effectiveness. There needs to be a process for evaluating board member performance and making recommendations regarding their future service with the board.

5. Too small. Sometimes a board is ineffective because it is simply too small in number. When we consider the awesome responsibilities of board leadership, it's easy to see why we need enough people to do the work. While it is difficult to specify an appropriate size for all boards, in general, a board should range in number from 11 to 21 members. We need enough members to lead and form the core of the committees and, in general, share in the other work of the board. We also need sufficient numbers to reflect the desired diversity in the board as well as assure the range of viewpoints that spurs innovation and creativity in board planning and decision-making.

6. Lack of functioning committee structure. Lack of a functioning committee structure is another reason why boards fail to perform at an acceptable level. While it is true that major decisions are made in board meetings, it is also true that most of the work that supports and implements this decision-making occurs at the committee level. If the board has a committee structure that functions inadequately, this can lead to poor performance in general.

7. No strategic plan. Lack of a strategic plan, in most cases, will also lead to poor board performance. If the organization lacks a strategic plan that provides clear direction so critical in this period of rapid change the board can spend significant amounts of time talking about topics that simply don't matter. Related to the absence of a strategic plan is lack of a long-range service delivery and financial development plan that will advance the strategic plan.

7. No plan for orientation of new and old members. Boards also fail because they have no plan for orientation of new and old members. Deliberate thought is rarely given to the matter of blending new and old board members into a well-functioning team. Related to this, is lack of a formal plan of board training and education to continually upgrade the level of board skills and knowledge.

Some of these problems will be painfully familiar you and the good news is they are all preventable!

Chapter 23: Non-profit Organisation's Board Development Process.

Building a more effective board is a process. As we know, things don't change overnight in organizations. It takes a commitment on the part of the leaders of a board to make it happen. The experience of other non-profits suggests that it can take 2-5 years to create an effective, self-renewing board. But if board members are willing to make the commitment, dramatic improvements are possible almost immediately by applying the proven techniques that follow.

1. Recruitment and nominations.

The first board development practice, and by far the most important, is having in place a board recruitment and nominations process. In contrast to the typical short-term recruitment process that focuses narrowly on filling anticipated board vacancies for the current year, the process described in this chapter helps to assure that there is a long-range plan for board leadership development.

This long-range plan for developing future board leadership centres on the following questions. Who will be serving on and leading the board over the next five years? What is our plan to scout board leadership talent for the future? How will we go about fostering and developing future board leadership? What we are really talking about here is extending the timeline for board development and recruitment activities. In many organizations, board recruitment and nominations activities are really ad hoc in nature. Typical bylaw language describes a process in which the board president appoints a nominations committee whose short-term task is to recruit candidates that will fill a specified number of vacancies at the upcoming annual meeting.

Below are some of the characteristics of a longer-range developmental process.

a. Year-round committee. Because board recruitment and nominations is such an important activity, we need to begin by looking at it as a year-round committee function instead of the traditional ad hoc nominations process. Reflecting this long-range focus, many boards are changing the name of their Nominations Committee to the Board Development Committee because developing leaders includes more than nominating people to serve on our boards. It's truly a year-round function; prospecting, contacting, recruiting, orienting, supporting, providing ongoing training, and evaluating.

b. Link to the strategic plan. It is important to match board recruitment and development activities with the new requirements and demands of the strategic plan. The ideal time to do this is right after the strategic planning process has been completed. The board reviews the mission, vision, goals and strategies, and then determines any new skills, knowledge, personal contacts and other attributes future board members will need to possess in order for the board to do its part in advancing the strategic plan.

c. Profile of the current board. At the same time, we need to analyze the current shape of the board. The Board Development Committee can create a profile of the current board using a matrix designed for this purpose. Key factors that define sought-after expertise, knowledge, skills, experience, as well as relevant demographic factors are arranged along the top of the matrix. The names of current board members are listed down the side of the matrix. The Committee then uses the matrix to complete the profile.

d. Focused recruiting priorities. By reviewing the agency strategic plan as well as the profile of current board strengths and weaknesses, the Board Development Committee identifies the gap between the skills and knowledge needed on the board, and what board members currently possess. Based on this analysis, the Board Development Committee can now set clear recruiting priorities for future board recruitment.

e. Written member job description. Another key element in the board development process is a written board member job description. For a board to operate successfully each member must understand and accept the specific duties and responsibilities that come with board membership. More and more organizations have found it helpful to develop a written statement of agreement for board members. This statement serves as a job description and clarifies board responsibilities. The job description, in very clear language, sets forth the expectations the organization has of its board members. The most effective job descriptions are those that state in behavioural terms precisely what board members are expected to do.

For most organizations, key responsibilities include the following; consistently attendance at regular board meetings, participation as an active member of at least one committee, participation in the fund-raising activities of the organization in a manner appropriate for that board member, as well as preparation in advance before regular board meetings by reading and studying materials sense in advance regarding key actions the board is expected to take at the next meeting. In addition, many organizations now expect their board members to attend an annual board planning or education event sometimes held on an evening, or a weekend. While there is no one right way to develop a job description, the format that you choose should cover some of the expectations listed above.

This written job description which should be periodically reviewed and updated by the Board of Directors, is the critical tool in recruitment of new board members. Like anyone contemplating a serious volunteer commitment, prospective board members want to know what is expected of them along with an estimate of the required time. Avoid the temptation to downplay the responsibilities of board membership. New board members will eventually find out what the true expectations are and if they are different from what they were told before coming on to the board; that is not good. It includes some of the basic expectations that most organizations have for their board members. It is not intended to serve the needs of every organization; consider the starting point in the design of a job description that matches your needs.

2. The Executive Committee

Another critical element in board effectiveness is a functioning executive committee. In most organizations in the U.S, the Executive committee consists of the four executive officers of the Board; the president, vice-president, secretary, and treasurer. Sometimes other members of the board are included as part of the Executive committee; for example chairs of the standing committees or at-large members from the board to assure representation of diverse viewpoints.

The Executive committee plays three critical roles; planning the agenda of board meetings, making decisions on behalf of the full board, and serving as a communication link with other members of the board, especially the committee chairs.

a. Planning the agenda of board meetings. It is the responsibility of the Executive committee to meet regularly before board meetings with the Executive Director to develop the board meeting agenda.

117

b. Making decisions on behalf of the full board. In between the regular meetings of the board, the Executive committee, during its own meeting, is able to make decisions that can't wait for the next regular board meeting or on matters that the full board has delegated authority to the Executive committee. In both cases, the Executive committee receives its authority from the full board and needs to report on its decision-making at the subsequent meeting of the board.

c. Serving as a communication link with other members of the board. In order to be effective, the board must foster communication among its members in between regular meetings. The executive committee can play a vital role to ensure that this happens utilizing telephone, fax and email.

To facilitate its work, the executive committee should meet on a regular basis. For example, if the board holds its regular meetings on monthly basis, the executive committee might also meet monthly in between the regular board meetings. The president and executive director should develop an agenda for the executive committee in advance of its meetings.

Here is a process that will assist the executive committee. When the executive director and board president meet, they should begin by identifying agenda items that can be appropriately handled by the executive committee itself. These items would be placed on the executive committee's meeting agenda than as action items. In placing such items in this category, board president and executive director are assuming, based on past practice as well as relevant bylaw language and board policy, that such items are appropriate for executive committee decision-making. The next agenda category includes those items that would be appropriate for executive committee discussion and or referral to the full board as action items or as information items. In this instance, the Board President and Executive Director are making the judgment that the executive committee lacks authority to act directly on such items. Their discussion of such items during the executive committee meeting may lead to recommendations for future action by the board as a whole but the executive committee will stop short of making a decision on its own.

A third category of executive committee meeting agenda items would be those items that are offered to executive committee members for their information only; they don't require action by the executive committee or by the board as a whole, but the Board President and Executive Director consider this information as important enough to share with other members of the executive committee.

By working with an executive committee agenda organized in this manner, the members will use their meeting time much more effectively and efficiently, resulting in decisions on matters that are appropriate for executive committee action. More importantly, they will lay the groundwork for effective decision-making by the board as a whole by reviewing, and if appropriate, making recommendations for board action for items that must be handled by the full

Board of Directors. They will also avoid spending unnecessary time on information items that require no real discussion or board deliberation.

As a result of such a meeting process, the executive committee can then construct an agenda for the full board meeting that places priority on action items. It can be seen that by taking care of its own work in an effective way, the executive committee facilitates effective decision-making by the board as a whole.

Chapter 24: Non-profit Organisation's Board Committee Structure.

An effective committee structure helps to increase the involvement of board members because it gives them an opportunity to use their skills and experience. They provide a training ground for future leaders both for individuals who are currently board members as well as non-board members who may be asked to serve on the board in the future. They increase the visibility and outreach of the organization by including non-board members in committee membership. Committees provide a means for information to flow from the community, clients, and line staff to the board. Committees also give members the chance to freely and discuss issues in an informal setting. Finally, committees serve as excellent problem-solving and decision-making groups because of their small size.

There are at least 5 elements of committee effectiveness.

1. Written Committee Description. First, there should be a written description of what is expected of each committee to guide the chair and members. The description should summarize the purpose of the committee, its composition and selection procedure, and the specific duties of the committee.

2. An effective committee chair. The next element is an effective chairperson. In general, the committee chair should be a board member. This helps to ensure that the leadership of the committee is "in sync" with that of the Board as a whole. In seeking an effective chair, we are looking for two things; content knowledge and experience relevant to the work of the committee as well as proven leadership and people skills that will be essential if the committee is to work effectively.

Depending on the size of the organization, the committee chair will be responsible for preparing agendas for the meetings, assigning responsibilities to committee members and doing some of the follow-up to make sure assigned work is being done by members. In some instances, paid professional staff may be assigned to assist the committee chair but this is not always the case.

3. Members thoughtfully appointed. The next element of committee effectiveness is members who have been thoughtfully appointed. Each standing committee is generally composed of a core of five to eight members. They can be a mix of board and non-board members and should be recruited with the following question in mind. What tasks is the committee responsible for and who among our members and supporters possess the skills and experience needed to complete those tasks? As is the case with other forms of volunteer recruitment, every effort should be made to match the needs and requirements of the committee and the skills, knowledge and interests of prospective committee members. In many cases, prospective board members, as part of the recruitment process, will be given information about the board committee structure with suggestions on where they might best fit. For example, a prospective board member who has much skill and experience in fundraising would most likely be asked to serve on the fund development committee. In the end however, regardless of the preferences of board leaders, the individual board members should be able to select the committee assignment that they feel will best meet their needs, while at the same time, meeting the needs of the organization.

4. Accountability to the board. The next element of committee effectiveness is clear accountability to the Board of Directors. This begins with a written committee description that describes what the board expects from the committee. There should also be an effort to link the committee description with relevant strategic plan language. Again, using the fund development committee as an example, the committee description would reflect a major goal and supporting strategies that address the issue of agency funding. Under the umbrella of the funding goal and strategies, committee leadership would develop an annual fundraising strategy and supporting work plan in line with the funding strategic goal. This work plan would contain objectives incorporating measurable outcomes, and these measurable outcomes would be the basis for regular reporting of the committee to the board as a whole.

5. Well run meetings. The last element of committee effectiveness is well run meetings. In a sense, if a committee reflects the first five indicators of effectiveness, a clear description of its work, a chair that knows how to lead, a solid match between the interests, skills and experience of individual members on the one hand, and the needs and requirements of the committee on the other, a good mix of board and non-board members, and direct accountability to the board; we will have the makings of excellent committee meetings. It will still be important to provide for meeting space that matches the needs of the group, a written meeting agenda and any necessary information mailed out to members in advance of the meeting.

The organization, as part of the overall board education and training program, should also be prepared to provide training to committee members to help them sharpen their skills.

Chapter 25: Non-profit Organisation's Annual Board Self-evaluation Process.

A well-planned recruitment process and an effective committee structure lays the ground work for improved board performance; however, every so often the board as a whole needs to step back and look at itself. A process for board self-evaluation will help to maintain a high level of performance. It happens informally when directors get together and talk about individual and board concerns. But a formal process is also necessary. Notice that we are speaking of "self evaluation" of the board. In order to maximize board member commitment to the process, it is important that they are actors in the assessment process, rather than the passive recipients of someone else's evaluation of their performance.

An effective board evaluation process includes the following features.

1. Annual process. An effective process for self-evaluation of the board will be conducted on a regular or yearly basis. A good time is mid way into the board year by then, board members have had an opportunity to demonstrate their commitment and enough time remains to take corrective action if necessary.

2. Two-way Communication. In order to have board member support for the process, the evaluation will need to be viewed as a vehicle for two-way communication to provide feedback on performance to individual board members and also to solicit feedback from individual board members on the performance of a board as a whole and the level of support that they receive from their leaders as well as staff. A thorough evaluation would cover two areas; individual board member performance and a look at board and committee operations as a whole. Each board member should first be asked to assess their performance as a board member in critical areas such as input into policy and decision-making, committee participation, and fundraising. Board members should also be asked if there are any factors that have helped or hindered their performance. Finally they should be asked what they would need to maintain or increase their level of commitment.

3. Follow-through. An effective evaluation process will also lead to concrete plans for corrective action including a commitment on the part of the board to follow through so that the results of evaluation process lead to measurable improvements in board performance.

4. Board member accountability. The results of this assessment can then be used by the President and executive committee to determine which board members deserve positive feedback for acceptable performance and which board members, because of inadequate performance, need to be reminded of their responsibilities and finally, an effective evaluation process will relate directly to the overall board recruitment and nominations process. For example, a board member who has not followed through on commitments is unlikely to be asked by the Board Development Committee to run for a second term even though the bylaws may allow for this.

Chapter 26: Building an Effective Non-profit Board of Directors.

Every non-profit organization must have a Board of Directors. But, beyond this legal requirement, a well-informed and well-trained board is absolutely essential. An effective non-profit board of directors has a clear understanding of its roles and responsibilities. Board members, in effect, own the organization. They are the final policy makers and they employ staff.

Non-profit board has three broad areas of responsibilities; planning and policy development; community and organizational development; and, fundraising and support development.

The first, planning and policy development, includes determining the mission and vision that charts the future direction of the organization. This is usually accomplished through the board's leadership and participation in strategic planning. The first area covers policy development in response to major issues that are or will in the future have significant impact on the agency and the constituencies it serves. Also included is monitoring the performance of agency programs, products and services.

The second area, community and organizational development, means broadening the organization's base of support in the community; interacting with the community to bring new issues, opportunities and community needs to the attention of organization; maintaining accountability to the public, funders, members, and clients. It also includes training and developing current and new leaders within the board and committees, and assuring that the same development is occurring within the professional staff through the leadership of the Executive Director.

The third area, fundraising and support development, includes giving personal time and money; developing donors, members, and supporters; leading and supporting fundraising campaigns and events as well as maintaining accountability to donors and funders.

These three areas are closely linked to each other; if the Board is going to make decisions that reflect the true interests and needs of the organization's constituents, board members must be in tune with those constituents and the wider community of which they are part. If the Board is expected to raise funds to support the programs and services of the organization, then board members must be involved in planning and decision-making in meaningful ways so as to feel in a strong sense of individual and collective ownership. If the organization is counting on board members to raise funds from the community, then board members need to maintain relationships with individuals and institutions in that community.

Chapter 27: Summary of Roles and Responsibilities of Directors and Boards

Board of Directors are appointed to act on behalf of the shareholders to run the day to day affairs of the business. The board are directly accountable to the shareholders and each year the company will hold an annual general meeting (AGM) at which the directors must provide a report to shareholders on the performance of the company, what its future plans and strategies are and also submit themselves for re-election to the board.

The objects of the company are defined in the Memorandum of Association and regulations are laid out in the Articles of Association.

The board of directors' key purpose is to ensure the company's prosperity by collectively directing the company's affairs, whilst meeting the appropriate interests of its shareholders and stakeholders. In addition to business and financial issues, boards of directors must deal with challenges and issues relating to corporate governance, corporate social responsibility and corporate ethics.

It is important that board meetings are held periodically so that directors can discharge their responsibility to control the company's overall situation, strategy and policy, and to monitor the exercise of any delegated authority, and so that individual directors can report on their particular areas of responsibility.

Every meeting must have a chair, whose duties are to ensure that the meeting is conducted in such a way that the business for which it was convened is properly attended to and that all those entitled to may express their views and that the decisions taken by the meeting adequately reflect the views of the meeting as a whole. The chair will also very often decide upon the agenda and might sign off the minutes on his or her own authority.

Individual directors have only those powers which have been given to them by the board. Such authority need not be specific or in writing and may be inferred from past practice; however, the board as a whole remains responsible for actions carried out by its authority and it should therefore ensure that executive authority is only granted to appropriate persons and that adequate reporting systems enable it to maintain overall control.

The chairman of the board is often seen as the spokesperson for the board and the company.

The ultimate control as to the composition of the board of directors rests with the shareholders, who can always appoint and more importantly, sometimes dismiss a director. The shareholders can also fix the minimum and maximum number of directors; however, the board can usually appoint (but not dismiss) a director to his office as well. A director may be dismissed from office by a majority vote of the shareholders, provided that a special procedure is followed. The procedure is complex, and legal advice will always be required.

A Summary of roles of the board of directors

1. Establish vision, mission and values.
   a. Determine the company's vision and mission to guide and set the pace for its current operations and future development.
   b. Determine the values to be promoted throughout the company.
   c. Determine and review company goals.
   d. Determine company policies.

2. Set strategy and structure.
   a. Review and evaluate present and future opportunities, threats and risks in the external environment and current and future strengths, weaknesses and risks relating to the company.
   b. Determine strategic options, select those to be pursued, and decide the means to implement and support them.
   c. Determine the business strategies and plans that underpin the corporate strategy.
   d. Ensure that the company's organisational structure and capability are appropriate for implementing the chosen strategies.

3. Delegate to management.
   a. Delegate authority to management, and monitor and evaluate the implementation of policies, strategies and business plans.

    b. Determine monitoring criteria to be used by the board.

    c. Ensure that internal controls are effective.

    d. Communicate with senior management.

4. Exercise accountability to shareholders and be responsible to relevant stakeholders.

    a. Ensure that communications both to and from shareholders and relevant stakeholders are effective.

    b. Understand and take into account the interests of shareholders and relevant stakeholders.

    c. Monitor relations with shareholders and relevant stakeholders by gathering and evaluation of appropriate information.

    d. Promote the goodwill and support of shareholders and relevant stakeholders.

A Summary of responsibilities of directors.

1. Directors look after the affairs of the company, and are in a position of trust. They might abuse their position in order to profit at the expense of their company, and, therefore, at the expense of the shareholders of the company.

2. Consequently, the law imposes a number of duties, burdens and responsibilities upon directors, to prevent abuse. Much of company law can be seen as a balance between allowing directors to manage the company's business so as to make a profit, and preventing them from abusing this freedom.

3. Directors are responsible for ensuring that proper books of account are kept.

4. In some circumstances, a director can be required to help pay the debts of his company, even though it is a separate legal person. For example, directors of a company who try to 'trade out of difficulty' and fail may be found guilty of 'wrongful trading' and can be made personally liable. Directors are particularly vulnerable if they have acted in a way which benefits themselves.

    a. The directors must always exercise their powers for a 'proper purpose' that is, in furtherance of the reason for which they were given those powers by the shareholders.

    b. Directors must act in good faith in what they honestly believe to be the best interests of the company, and not for any collateral purpose. This means that, particularly in the event of a conflict of interest between the company's interests and their own, the directors must always favour the company.

    c. Directors must act with due skill and care.

    d. Directors must consider the interests of employees of the company.

Calling a directors' meeting.

A director, or the secretary at the request of a director, may call a directors' meeting. A secretary may not call a meeting unless requested to do so by a director or the directors. Each director must be given reasonable notice of the meeting, stating its date, time and place. Commonly, seven days is given but what is 'reasonable' depends in the last resort on the circumstances.

Non-executive directors.

Legally speaking, there is no distinction between an executive and non-executive director. Yet there is inescapably a sense that the non-executive's role can be seen as balancing that of the executive director, so as to ensure the board as a whole functions effectively. Where the executive director has an intimate knowledge of the company, the non-executive director may be expected to have a wider perspective of the world at large.

The chairman of the board.

The articles usually provide for the election of a chairman of the board. They empower the directors to appoint one of their own number as chairman and to determine the period for which he is to hold office. If no chairman is elected, or the elected chairman is not present within five minutes of the time fixed for the meeting or is unwilling to preside, those directors in attendance may usually elect one of their number as chairman of the meeting.

The chairman will usually have a second or casting vote in the case of equality of votes. Unless the articles confer such a vote upon him, however, a chairman has no casting vote merely by virtue of his office.

Since the chairman's position is of great importance, it is vital that his election is clearly in accordance with any special procedure laid down by the articles and that it is unambiguously minuted; this is especially important to avoid disputes as to his period in office. Usually there is no special procedure for resignation. As for removal, articles usually empower the board to remove the chairman from office at any time. Proper and clear minutes are important in order to avoid disputes.

Role of the chairman.

The chairman's role includes managing the board's business and acting as its facilitator and guide. This can includes.

    a. Determining board composition and organisation.

    b. Clarifying board and management responsibilities.

    c. Planning and managing board and board committee meetings.

    d. Developing the effectiveness of the board.

Shadow directors.

In many circumstances, the law applies not only to a director, but to a 'shadow director'. A shadow director is a person in accordance with whose directions or instructions the directors of a company are accustomed to act. Under this definition, it is possible that a director, or the whole board, of a holding company, and the holding company itself, could be treated as a shadow director of a subsidiary.

Professional advisers giving advice in their professional capacity are specifically excluded from the definition of a shadow director in the companies legislation.

Boards are responsible for strategy and compliance. The roles and responsibilities of directors are significantly different from those of managers and the job of a non-executive is a particular challenge.

Chapter 28: Conclusion

There are probably many more reasons to become a member of board director; but here are some of my primary thoughts.

1. Intellectual Challenge

According to a study, 54% of directors said that their primary motivation for sitting on a board is intellectual stimulation and, in most cases, intellectual stimulation is what you will receive! Boards, by definition, focus on the big picture of the company. This includes strategic planning, CEO succession planning, merger and acquisition and IT strategy. These are complex and multi-faceted subjects with major implications and thereby requiring immersion and effort. Furthermore, as a board director, your engagement will be on a part-time basis and as such the intellectual challenge will be magnified.

2. Career Development

As a board director, you will get exposure not only to a company different than the one you work at (assuming you are not retired) but it is possible that you will learn about a new industry and perhaps even experience the functioning of a business in a novel and particular geography. The size and stage of the company which you are a director of may also be inconsistent to that which you are accustomed. This variance will provide opportunity to develop your skills, experience and competencies.

Additionally, in many companies sitting on an outside board is a precursor to becoming CEO or other major line responsibilities.

3. Networking

If governance is done right, your board seat will provide you with a whole new set of contacts. In the not so distant past, a board seat might be just another venue in which to engage with other senior executives you already know or have at least a passing familiarity with. Today, most boards are far more heterogeneous and thus an excellent opportunity to expand your network and it will not be expanded with just anyone. Those you meet in the boardroom will be similarly accomplished and astute individuals who should enrich you both around the boardroom table and beyond.

4. Business Development

This should not be misinterpreted but simply put, being on a board will raise your profile. This can result in some indirect improvement to your business or career. In this case it is important to be mindful of potential conflicts but for the sake of comprehensiveness this is a dividend worth thinking about.

5. Giving Back

Some view board service as an opportunity to give back. This can be particularly true in the case of start-up or smaller company boards. In these cases, compensation may be minimal or even non-existent thus the main motivation is providing your expertise and experience to facilitate the growth and success of a business. In the case of non-profits, this is of course, the main motivation.

6. Prestige

Who can deny the cachet that comes along with being a board director? However, I mention this last deliberately. If you are interested in board service simply because of the perceived prominence it provides, think again. Being a good board director is a lot of work and responsibility. It is not simply a "feel good" opportunity but rather a job with specific roles and responsibilities including legal, fiduciary and ethical.

It is no secret that board service is gratifying and a goal for many. The reasons for this, as seen above, are ample and varied. Conversely, the responsibilities are real and can be quite significant. Insight and information will go a long way to equip you appropriately.

Good Luck!!

Made in the USA
San Bernardino, CA
22 August 2016